11-1-73

ATTITUDE CHANGE

AND

SOCIAL INFLUENCE

BASIC TOPICS IN PSYCHOLOGY

Edwin G. Boring, EDITOR

SOCIAL PSYCHOLOGY

LEONARD BERKOWITZ
The Development of Motives and Values in the Child

ARTHUR R. COHEN
Attitude Change and Social Influence

MORTON DEUTSCH AND ROBERT M. KRAUSS
Theories in Social Psychology

BERTRAM H. RAVEN
Interpersonal Relations and Behavior in Groups

ATTITUDE CHANGE AND SOCIAL INFLUENCE

Arthur R. Cohen

FOREWORD BY *Leon Festinger* AND *Philip Zimbardo*

Basic Books, Inc.

PUBLISHERS

NEW YORK : LONDON

Ninth Printing

© 1964 by Basic Books, Inc.
Library of Congress Catalog Card Number: 64–22400
Manufactured in the United States of America
DESIGNED BY VINCENT TORRE

EDITOR'S FOREWORD

THE ENORMOUS GROWTH of scientific research and activity since World War II has included psychology as one of the recognized life sciences. Psychology now makes no small contribution to the rapid change in Western culture and civilization, a contribution that consists of a stream of new discoveries. There is also to be remembered, however, psychology's contribution to its own maintenance. That lies in teaching, for every academic generation must train the next. The roots of psychology must grow if the branches are to spread and the seeds of new growth germinate in the classroom. Research would ultimately exhaust itself were adequate prior training of the scientists deficient. That fact is now well recognized in principle, if not always in practice.

These short books are designed, in the first place, to make instruction easier. The ablest instructor is inevitably an individualist. He is never content to design his course to fit the idiosyncrasies of the other able man who wrote his textbook. A single text, moreover, seldom contains enough material to constitute all the reading a student needs. The instructor will wish to supplement his text and lectures and to have freedom in choosing what he shall add. The availability of many small books packed with solid reading enables the instructor to choose what he wants and makes their purchase by the student practicable.

The other use of these books is to satisfy the intellectual curiosity of intelligent laymen. They are not so technical that professional men and thinking women who are keeping an eye on the advance of civilization cannot use them to understand what the psychologists think and know. The philosopher, the historian, the lawyer, the physician, and the modern mother of grown children can surely employ these books in keeping up with the scientific times.

Since World War II, psychology has been expanding in many directions, forming connections with social science, on the one side, and with biological and physical science, on the other. It has thus been said to be both "sociotropic" and "biotropic" as it turns now toward social science, now toward biological science. Scientific biology is older than scientific sociology, and thus biotropic psychology is older than sociotropic. As a consequence of its youth, scientific social psychology is at present less sure of itself than is physiological psychology or psychophysics, and for that reason Basic Topics in Social Psychology tend to stress the way in which facts are a function of method, to discuss how the facts were obtained, and sometimes to present contradictory findings. Such contradictions are no fault of the author, but rather that of the youthfulness of this science. With social psychology still waiting on maturity, these books give their readers an insight into a science that is still growing up.

Edwin G. Boring

FOREWORD

ARTHUR R. COHEN died on July 10, 1963. About two weeks before his death he finished making the last changes in the manuscript of this book and returned it to the editor. It was, as it turns out, the final work in a highly creative and productive career. He was thirty-six years old when he died.

One of us was a member of the faculty of the University of Michigan when Cohen was a graduate student there, the other a graduate student at Yale University who did his Ph.D. thesis under Cohen's supervision. Thus, perhaps we can say something about him and his career.

Social psychology, at the close of the 1940's, was a particularly exciting field for Cohen. Three major traditions, all strongly represented at the University of Michigan, came together to give him a unique combination of influences. Theodore Newcomb, who had worked at Columbia University with Gardner Murphy and Otto Klineberg; Daniel Katz, who had helped in the pioneering works of Floyd Allport at Syracuse University; and the members of the Research Center for Group Dynamics, who continued in the tradition of Kurt Lewin, all had their impact on Cohen.

In this intellectual environment Cohen combined these points of view with his own talent and ability to emerge as a theoretically creative, methodologically sophisticated, and highly knowledgeable social psychologist.

One further influence was to have a considerable effect on Cohen. His first job brought him to Yale University, where he worked closely with Carl Hovland on research in communication and attitude change. Hovland, with a background and tradition from learning theory different from that Cohen had at Michigan, gave him greater critical insight into the field. There was, and is, probably no one who came closer to combining within himself all the major strengths and traditions in modern social psychology.

Cohen's research always focused on the question of how attitudes change, but his breadth reflected itself in the variety of ways he approached the problem. Inquiries into the needs of people for structuring their cognition, into the relation of personality variables to attitude change, into the role of motivation interacting with attitudes all revealed his continual attempts to integrate his field of inquiry. This research was always imaginative and interesting. Thus, whether he was being stimulated by problems in group dynamics, by the theory of cognitive dissonance, or by questions of the application of learning theory to attitude change, he always brought his own originality to bear in making a novel contribution.

He was strongly and idealistically committed to his field of scientific investigation. This gave him two important qualities which he communicated to students and colleagues alike: a rich enthusiasm for his subject matter and a penetrating critical appraisal of work that did not come quite up to his standards. Because of this, the influence Cohen has had on his contemporaries was fully as great as the influence his teachers had on him. Many of the active research workers in the field today, including ourselves, owe him a debt of intellectual gratitude.

This book reflects all these things about Arthur R. Cohen. It is an attempt to integrate and organize in a systematic manner all that is now known concerning attitude change. Only someone with the breadth and scope Cohen had could do this job.

Throughout the book may be seen the evidences of Cohen's enthusiasm, broad knowledge, and appreciation for the connection between theory and data. Throughout may also be seen the critical ability with which he can shed light on rather murky areas. But above all, what Cohen accomplishes is a constructive and creative contribution to the field.

Our guess is that this book will continue to be useful and to live for many years—thus extending the life of our colleague.

Leon Festinger
Philip Zimbardo

Stanford University
May 1964

PREFACE

How ARE people's minds changed? Who changes, and why? These questions are not new. For centuries principles of rhetoric based on logic and insight have been taught to students, speakers, and writers. Reformers, politicians, policemen, propagandists, educators, club members, and others have always been concerned with the conditions under which people can be influenced to accept new ideas and to cast off old ways of thought. Only within the past twenty years, however—since World War II— have the principles and assumptions gathered through experience and common-sense observation been put to the test of controlled research.

The present volume brings together and summarizes much of the evidence that research has provided on the general topics of attitude change and social influence. In a sense it records progress toward a scientific analysis of rhetoric through the investigation of basic psychological processes. Most of the research cited applies precise, controlled experimentation to the study of the principal areas in the field of persuasion, analyzing the effectiveness of arguments and appeals, the personality factors underlying the acceptance of influence, the effects of social roles and interactions, and similar issues, in terms of principles of learning, perception, motivation, and cognition. Although the investigators whose research we shall examine differ considerably in their theoretical orientations and in the specific problems they have chosen to study, they are all concerned with the modification of attitudes and beliefs through communication and social interaction and with the relevance of the principles thus derived for social influence in everyday life.

This volume focuses on the immediate and direct ways in which persuasive communications and the members of a person's social group come to influence the attitudes he holds. In carrying out this aim, it has been necessary to forego discussing a number of critical issues which are essential for a complete understanding of the process of attitude change. This book does not take up the definition and conceptualization of attitude, but instead assumes that there is a commonly accepted core of meaning for the term "attitude change" which can serve as a working basis in the present review. This core of meaning rests, of course, on formulations as to how attitudes are formed and acquired, how to scale and measure them, how to design experiments, how to manipulate variables, how society influences persons in their social roles, how organizations and institutions make contact with the persons they wish to influence, and why certain persons and groups hold certain opinions and not others. The reader who wishes to pursue any of these issues further will find a large body of relevant literature at his disposal. Attention here is concentrated on those psychological factors which are activated when a persuasive communication actually enters a person's psychological field. How are the communication's stimuli transformed and modified by perceptual, cognitive, learning, and motivational processes? What is the role of these processes in attitude change?

Chapters 1 and 2 open the discussion by introducing the formal aspects of communication: the effects on attitude change of the organization of the communication and the characteristics of the communicator. Next are considered the structure of rewards and punishments that affect the persuasiveness of a communication and the role played by the personality characteristics of the person toward whom the communication is directed. Chapter 5 begins the examination of the more subtle psychological processes underlying attitude change, with especial attention to the nature of psychological consistency and the determinants of conformity. Chapter 8 raises the problem of building resistance to persuasion, and Chapter 9 asks some fundamental questions and points out some directions for future research.

I take pleasure in expressing my great indebtedness to Isidor Chein for his thoughtful and invaluable critique of the entire manuscript. My thanks are also due to Jack W. Brehm and Charles W. Greenbaum for their comments on one or another portion of the text. Finally, I want to thank my wife Barbara for her encouragement, help, and advice at every stage of the preparation of this book.

A. R. C.

July 1963

CONTENTS

Contents

ATTITUDE CHANGE

AND

SOCIAL INFLUENCE

I

THE COMMUNICATION

THE EARLIEST studies of attitude and attitude change were made in the 1920's and 1930's. Investigators at that time were mainly interested in the degree to which different attitudes were held by different groups (for example, the attitudes toward the Spanish Civil War held by conservatives and liberals) and in the effects of exposure to media of communication as measured by responses to questionnaires that attempted to scale attitudes (the effects of lectures, pamphlets, and motion pictures on opinions). More recent investigators (for example, Sherif & Hovland, 1961) note that there was little concern with the psychological processes involved in the individual expression of attitudes and the pattern of stimulus conditions under which responses show change.

Since the 1930's there has been an increasing concern with the basic psychological processes underlying attitudes and their modification. The new trend got under way with the work of Hovland and his colleagues in the Information and Education Division of the War Department during World War II. Their program included a great variety of studies; of special interest here are those which employed controlled variation. These experiments were among the first to show how specific content transmitted by specific communicators affects particular audiences. Let us begin by describing some of the work done in this program and then broaden our discussion by including later work which stems from the initial investigations and which bears on similar and new theoretical and empirical problems.

The Effects of One-Sided versus Two-Sided Communications

What role does the organization of arguments play in the effectiveness of a persuasive appeal? In attempting to answer this question, writers have in the past dealt with methods of refutation, problems of emphasis, number of repetitions, and so forth. One of the central problems, however, is whether it is more effective to present only one side of an issue or to present both sides. Should a communicator concentrate only on the points supporting the position he advocates or should he also discuss opposing arguments? Which strategy is the more effective?

In *Experiments on Mass Communication,* the volume in which they report the results of their wartime studies, Hovland, Lumsdaine, and Sheffield (1949) investigate whether, when the weight of evidence supports the main thesis of a communication, it is more effective to present only the materials supporting the point at issue or to introduce opposing arguments as well.

These investigators presented to two experimental groups of 214 soldiers and to a control group of 197 soldiers communications on whether there would be an early end to the war with Japan after the surrender of Germany in 1945. All of the soldiers were tested some time before the communication on their beliefs about whether Japan would surrender. One experimental group was given a fifteen-minute talk that presented only the arguments supporting the idea that the war with Japan would be a long one; the talk included much factual material stressing Japan's strength. The other experimental group was given a communication which contained the same material plus an additional four minutes of information, woven into the presentation, which stressed the United States' advantages and Japan's weaknesses.

The investigators' hypothesis was that those soldiers who were given only a one-sided argument would distrust a presentation that had failed to include opposing arguments and would be stimulated to rehearse their own position and to seek new ways of supporting it. After the presentation of the material, the soldiers were again measured on their beliefs about the probable length of the war with Japan, and a measure of change from before to after the presentation was computed. The effectiveness of the program was evaluated by comparing the average change in each of the experimental groups with the changes in a control group which had heard no communication but had merely been given the "before" and "after" attitude measures at the same time as the experimental groups.

Both experimental programs were found to be extremely effective in producing change in the men's opinions, but neither program had any advantage over the other for the audience as a whole. Depending upon the initial position of the listener, however, the net effects were different for the two ways of presenting the material. The program giving both sides was more effective for those men initially opposed to the position advocated (those who expected a short war), whereas the program giving the one-sided picture was more effective for men initially favoring the stand taken (those who expected a long war).

The investigators also expected that an obviously one-sided communication would be less effective with well-educated men and that these men would be more likely to take seriously arguments that seem to take all the factors into account. Less well-educated men, on the other hand, with undeveloped skill in critical thinking, might be more impressed with the strength of a one-sided argument, without thinking of objections. These expectations were borne out: The program which presented both sides was more effective with the better-educated men, and the program which presented one side was more effective with the less educated.

When initial position and amount of education are considered together, the two-sided communication turned out to be more effective with better-educated men, no matter what their initial position, and the one-sided presentation most effective with those less-educated men already convinced of the position advocated. Thus, to decide the most effective type of presentation requires information about the educational level of the audience and the beliefs that audience already holds.

Do these two types of communication reveal differences in resistance to counterinfluence? A further experiment (Lumsdaine & Janis, 1953) bears directly on this point. In this experiment, a week after having been exposed to either a one-sided or a two-sided communication on Russia's inability to produce atomic bombs for many years to come, half of the subjects in each experimental group were exposed to a counterargument before being asked to state their opinions again. The counterpropaganda consisted of a playing-up and an elaboration of the arguments in the two-sided communication, as well as some new material. When the scores for change were examined, it was found that while there was no difference for those not exposed to the counterpropaganda, those who had been exposed to the counterpropaganda and who had heard the two-sided program were more resistant to the counterpropaganda than those who had heard only the one-sided argument.

In summarizing the results of these two experiments, Hovland, Janis, and Kelley (1953, p. 110) conclude that a two-sided communication is more effective in the long run when, no matter what its initial opinion, the audience is exposed to subsequent counterpropaganda or when, regardless of subsequent exposure, the audience initially disagrees with the position advocated by the communicator. The two-sided communication is less effective if the audience agrees with the initial position and is not exposed to later counterpropaganda. With respect to the second experiment, the two-sided argument apparently prepares the listener to meet counterarguments; it would thus seem especially effective in "inoculating" the listener against subsequent counterinfluence. "Inoculation" relates also to the problem of building up resistance to pressures toward attitude change (see Ch. 8).

The concept of inoculation also raises questions about the way in which two-sided communications present opposing arguments. Although the investigators are most interested in resolving the issue of which type of communication is the more effective, their results make it clear that further work should take account of the manner in which opposing arguments are introduced, the character of the arguments, and the extent to which they are explicitly refuted. Some of these questions are considered in Chapter 8, and their investigation increases our understanding of the conditions under which two-sided communications are most effective as well as those under which refutation can be successful.

The foregoing conclusions about the relative effectiveness of one-sided and two-sided communications have been extended by other investigators (Thistlethwaite & Kamenetsky, 1955). Attitude change tends to be greater for those subjects whose comprehension of the communicator's conclusion is greater or who show fewer and less intense discounting reactions to the communication. Introducing facts in support of the "other side" leads to less change of attitude when the facts are unfamiliar to the subjects, but failure to include well-known facts on the "other side" also weakens the appeal. Thus, to the degree that the facts included in the different communications are comprehensible and familiar, the appeals will be differentially effective in producing changes in attitude.

The experiments cited take little account of the fact that the persons subjected to attempts at influence are not merely members of an audience but also persons with active social lives within their social groups. Festinger (1955) has commented on the fact that knowledge about the effect of interpersonal and group processes implies that such processes may be modifying the effects obtained by one-sided versus two-sided arguments. It is possible that the two-sided presentation, by stressing the controversial aspect of the problem, may set off considerable discussion among the listeners in the week-long interval after hearing it. Thus, rather than showing the effectiveness of a one-sided versus a two-sided presentation, the results may show the resistance to counterinfluence under one set of conditions, where opinions are not anchored in a membership group, as compared to the resistance under conditions where they are firmly anchored in a membership group. The investigators mentioned, as well as many others, are aware of the importance of these interactions among persons, and in Chapter 7 we shall consider how such interactions operate to modify and to produce effects on social influence and attitude change.

The Effects of Stating a Conclusion

Whether a conclusion should be stated conspicuously in a persuasive communication is a question which has long been argued by propagandists, educators, and public speakers. Is it more effective to let an audience draw its own conclusion, or is it better to make the conclusion explicit? If we assume that indirect suggestion is more effective or that decisions are more effective when reached independently, we might expect the presentation of an implicit conclusion to be the more powerful. But some persons, especially the less intelligent, will miss the conclusion entirely if it is not stated explicitly.

Hovland and Mandell (1952) designed an experiment for studying this problem systematically. They compared two types of communication which were identical in every respect except one: in the first, the communicator drew the conclusion at the end, while in the second the conclusion was left to the audience. Under the first set of conditions, the general principles of the relevant topic (current economic issues) were presented, together with a statement of the existing situation (the bad financial status of the U.S.). From the principles and the statement of the situation, a logical conclusion could be drawn by the individual listener (desirability of devaluation of American currency). Under the second set of conditions, the implication and conclusion were stated explicitly by the communicator. The results showed that more than twice as many listeners changed their opinions in the direction advocated by the communicator when the conclusion was explicitly drawn as did when it was left to the audience.

While these results favor stating the conclusion explicitly, it does not follow that this strategy will invariably be superior. A number of factors are involved: the kind of communicator (whether he is trustworthy, an expert, or seen as biased), the kind of audience (their intelligence, sophistication, types of personality), the kind of issue (whether or not it is "ego-involving," how complex it is), and the degree of explicitness with which the conclusion is actually drawn. Research to be presented later (see Ch. 2) deals with the effects of credibility and trustworthiness on attitude change. Here we may note that later research (Thistlethwaite, de Haan, & Kamenetsky, 1955) explores the role of intelligence in the effectiveness of stating conclusions. Stating the conclusions in the message proves to be more effective in changing the opinions of the less intelligent members of the audience than it does those of the more intelligent.

In general, however, later research has been unable to confirm these earlier findings. One set of investigators used as an issue the wisdom of the United States in following a policy of limited war in Korea. They obtained positive results, but other investigators suggest that these results may have been due to the fact that the measures of attitude emphasized comprehension of what the speaker said rather than personal attitudes about the issue. These critics base this interpretation on their finding that under conditions where the conclusions were stated, the subjects showed an increase in comprehension of the material over those where the conclusions were left implicit, but the two groups showed no difference in agreement with the position advocated. An alternative explanation for these conflicting results (suggested by Krech, Crutchfield, & Ballachey, 1962) is that the complexity of an issue is a central factor in the effectiveness of stating a conclusion (Hovland *et al.,* 1953). The issue of limited war in Korea was one which had been widely discussed in the mass media, so that the arguments pro and con had already been spelled out for the subjects in understandable terms. By contrast, the issue of currency devaluation is a complex economic problem which most people do not understand very well.

In summary, then, we may state that persuasive communications which present a complicated and unfamiliar series of arguments on impersonal topics to less intelligent people are more effective when the conclusion is stated explicitly than when the audience is left to draw its own conclusion. There are, however, many problems that remain to be investigated before we understand fully the conditions under which explicit presentations are more effective than implicit ones in producing attitude change.

The Effects of Order of Presentation

The sequence of presentation of the arguments is another important aspect of a persuasive communication. Should one start with his strongest arguments or save them until the end? Different orders of presentation in persuasive communications are discussed by Hovland, Janis, and Kelley in *Communication and Persuasion* (1953). They divide the problem into two parts: (1) When only a single side of an issue is presented, is it more effective to utilize the strongest arguments at the outset or at the end? (2) When both sides of an issue are presented successively, does the side presented first or the side presented last have the advantage?

After reviewing the evidence as to the difference between a "climax" order (important arguments reserved until the end) and an "anticlimax" order (major arguments presented at the beginning and weaker ones at the end), the investigators conclude that it is unlikely that one or the other order of presentation will invariably turn out to be superior. Rather, they feel that different external factors will produce different outcomes, and they suggest what sorts of factor will affect the outcome. Most important are attention, learning, and acceptance. They say further that the presentation of major arguments at the outset (anticlimax order) will be most effective when the audience is initially little interested in the communication, for it helps to catch attention. But when attention and motivation to learn are present, they hypothesize that the climax order will be more effective in gaining acceptance because the anticlimax order fails to fulfill the expectations created by the initial portions of the communication and may produce a letdown that promotes forgetting. Thus the advantages of one order over the other depends on the particular conditions under which the communication is presented, including the predispositions of the audience and the type of material being communicated.

Which order is the more effective when both sides of an issue are presented? This second problem of sequence is known in psychology as the "primary–recency" question. It was first stated in its most general form as "Is there a Law of Primacy in persuasion?" An early study (Lund, 1925) made on college students, in which an instructor communicated two sides of an issue, argued for such a law. This "law" stated that the side of an issue presented first will be more persuasive than the side presented subsequently. In considering the evidence from later experiments, Hovland, Janis, and Kelley (1953) conclude that neither primacy nor recency produces consistent effects. They argue for research on the factors that contribute to the differences in results that have been obtained in the various experiments. These factors may include the complex and interacting roles of learning, attention, and acceptance, and the role of such special factors as the position of a teacher as communicator to his own students in a classroom.

Following up this line of attack, a later volume by Hovland and his colleagues (*The Order of Presentation in Persuasion*, 1957) presents replications of earlier experiments and a number of new experiments on the effects of order. Instead of attempting to confirm a general law of primacy in persuasion, they ask what conditions make either primacy or recency effective in persuasion. One set of studies tests the generality and validity of the Law of Primacy; a second deals with the effects of different sequences of appeals and arguments within a single communication.

Order of Successive Communications

The series of experiments on the effects of primacy and recency have led to the following generalizations (Hovland, 1957, pp. 130-138).

1. *The Law of Primacy is not general.* When two sides of an issue are presented successively by different communicators, the side presented first does not necessarily have the advantage. In a study by Hovland and Mandell, successive communica-

tions advocated first one and then the other side of an issue. The order of presentation was counterbalanced—half of the subjects received the "pro" arguments first and the other half the "anti" arguments first. The subjects were given opinion questionnaires after the first side had been presented and then again after the second side. The results failed to replicate the findings by Lund (1925): although some groups showed primacy effects, most groups showed recency effects. The authors speculate whether the differences between Lund's results and theirs may be due to differences in learning and acceptance. The motivation to learn the first communication may have been stronger in Lund's experimental group, and the subjects' commitment to the statement of their first opinion may have reinforced their acceptance of the first communication.

2. *Public commitment is a significant factor in the effects of primacy and recency.* If, after hearing only one side of a controversial issue, a listener makes a response which *publicly* indicates his position on the issue, the result is a primacy effect. Without telling the subjects that they would later hear the other side of a controversial issue, the investigators presented one side and asked half of the subjects to write for publication their opinions on the issue, while the other half were asked to write their opinions anonymously. Then the other side of the issue was presented to both groups and their opinions recorded again. The investigators found that the public expression of opinion tended to fix opinions on the first side and to make the presentation of the second side less effective in changing attitudes— a primacy effect. Where there is no public commitment (as in the Hovland and Mandell study), the mere statement of one's opinion anonymously on a questionnaire after hearing only one side of an issue does not reduce the effectiveness of the second side. The experimenters believe that the effect of public commitment is due to social rewards and the need for social approval. Having placed his opinions on record, the subject feels that he cannot alter his views if he is to be regarded as consistent and honest by those with whom he expects to interact.

3. *Primacy effects may occur when one communicator presents contradictory information in a single communication, but this effect can be reduced by interpolating other activities be-*

tween the two blocks of information and by warning the subjects against "the fallibility of first impressions." In a related
series of experiments, Luchins prepared two blocks of information describing the personality characteristics of a person not
known to the subjects. One block contained information about
an introverted person, the other block contained items characteristic of an extraverted person; for some subjects the order
was introversion–extraversion and for the other half the reverse. Subjects were then asked to select adjectives reflecting
their impressions, to write brief descriptions of personality, and
to make predictions about the later behavior of the person they
had read about. The material presented first proved to be
considerably more influential in determining what the subjects
thought to be the chief characteristics of the person described.
When subjects in a comparable experiment were forewarned
about the possible fallibility of first impressions before any information was presented, however, the second block of information tended to exert a relatively greater influence than
the first on the final impressions formed. Recency was most
effective in the group that was forewarned, next most effective
in another group in which the warning was interpolated between the first and second blocks of information, and weakest
in a third group for whom arithmetic tasks were interpolated
between the two blocks of information. In all three groups,
however, the recency effect was stronger than the primacy
effect.

Order within a Communication

What is the best way to organize the material when a complex argument for one side of an issue is to be presented? For
example, should you begin with those arguments which favor
your side of the issue and then refute the opposing arguments,
or should you take care of the opposition first?

1. *If a communicator first arouses the subject's needs and
then presents information that tends to satisfy those needs, the
information will be accepted more readily than if the arousal of
need follows the presentation of the information.* An experiment by Cohen compared two situations: one, presenting to
college students a threatening communication about problems

of grading and necessary reforms, was followed by the information that grading "on the curve" would solve the current situation; the other reversed the order of the presentation of the threat and the information about grading on the curve. Attitudes toward grading on the curve were measured before and immediately after the experimental introduction of the threat and the information, and then again three months later. It was found that the first sequence (need–information) was more effective, probably because the second order (information–need) did not make much sense to the subjects. Information presented after a need is aroused can operate in a direct fashion; less effort is required on the part of the listener to see it as relevant to his needs. Those who receive the information first do not see the point of the information as they are getting it. They see its relevance only afterward, and by then they may already have lost much of it because they have not been paying close attention; in any case, they now have the job of reconstructing what they have heard in a manner relevant to their needs.

2. *Attitudes change more when communications highly desirable to the subject are presented first, followed by the less desirable ones, than when the less desirable ones come first.* McGuire found that the communicator elicited more agreement with his views when his earlier communications were rewarding for the subject. McGuire's hypothesis is that, with this sequence, the subject starts out by becoming progressively more responsive to the communicator in terms of paying attention and being willing to learn; later the communicator capitalizes on these responses in the less rewarding part of the message. On the other hand, the communicator who first presents undesirable content to the recipient excites responses leading to nonacceptance (withdrawing attention) because agreeing with these undesirable issues is unpleasant; by the time he gets to the rewarding part of his message he has lost the subject's attention.

3. *The "pro–con" order is superior to the "con–pro" order when an authoritative communicator plans to mention "pro" arguments and also nonsalient "con" arguments.* This generalization comes from an experiment by Janis and Feierabend.

One experimental group received a version of a pamphlet on civil defense in which the arguments for civil defense were presented first, followed by the arguments against it; the other group received a version which reversed the order. To gauge the relative effectiveness of the two forms of the communication, the subjects were given a postcommunication questionnaire on their willingness to volunteer for civil defense. The data showed that the group which received the "pro" arguments first found the communication more persuasive than did those who received the "con" attitudes first: they were more ready to volunteer for civil defense. Janis and Feierabend interpret their results as an example of the resolution of an approach–avoidance conflict: arguments in favor of a position agreed with initially strengthen the approach tendency, and arguments against the position, provided they are not too strong, can then be handled without causing a reversal of the initially favorable attitude.

More recent research by Miller and Campbell (1959) and Anderson and Barrios (1961) is also relevant to the problem of order effects. Miller and Campbell call attention to the fact that the rate of forgetting diminishes over time; we forget most rapidly immediately after learning, and in successive equal time intervals we forget proportionately less and less of what is left. Thus, of two associations equally strong at a given moment, the older will decay less rapidly. From the properties of the curve of forgetting, certain predictions can be made and tested.

Miller and Campbell varied the order in which they presented opposing arguments (pro–con, con–pro) to college students. The communications were on an issue about which the subjects had little prior information and had formed no opinions (a trial involving a suit for damages), so that there was little contamination from previous learning, a condition not generally met in the earlier two-sided studies. In addition to varying the order, the investigators varied both the time interval between the opposing arguments (none and one week) and the time of testing the effect of the arguments (immediately after the second argument and one week later). The measure of attitude toward the defendant's case (the "con" side) and toward the plaintiff's (the "pro" side) also showed a significant recency effect, no matter which information was presented first, under the conditions most favorable to the emergence of a recency effect as predicted from the curve of forgetting. The last-heard argument is most effective when there is a long delay between the first and second communications (with maximal loss of memory for the first) coupled with an immediate measurement after the second communication (with minimal loss of memory for the second). The last-heard argument is least effective when the two presentations are contiguous (so that the temporal advantage for the second is minimal) and the testing is delayed (so that the relative lapses of time since the initial exposures become more and more nearly equal). On the basis of the learning curve, however, one would not expect that the first-heard argument would have the advantage even under the latter conditions, which are those least unfavorable to it. Nevertheless, under these conditions the first-heard argument turns out to be the stronger one. In other words, there is a primacy effect when it is given a chance to show itself.

Miller and Campbell point out that most of the earlier experimental studies involved conditions of contiguous presentation and immediate testing. Immediate testing is a condition in which the relative time lapse is at its greatest for the first-heard argument, so that any primacy effect there may be is canceled out by the time-advantage given to the second argument. The reader familiar with the relative effects of what are known in the general psychology of memory and forgetting as retroactive and proactive inhibition will realize that from the point of view of these effects the first-heard argument is probably under the greatest disadvantage when the presentations are contiguous. It is not surprising, therefore, that different experiments have shown inconsistent results (Hovland, 1957). Miller and Campbell (1959) conclude that the evidence cited by Hovland and his colleagues could be interpreted as consistent with an ever-present primacy effect, though the strength of this effect would necessarily vary with the experimental conditions peculiar to each of the studies and would frequently be masked by a recency effect.

Anderson and Barrios (1961) raise an interesting issue:

what happens when a subject receives a series of communications on a variety of topics from the same source, each communication being divisible into "pro" and "con" segments? Although the primacy effects are striking at first, they diminish as the series of communications progresses. The investigators point out that there are several possible explanations for this result. For one thing, the particular pattern of good and bad adjectives used in the later sets may have stimulated an increased tendency to take account of all the words in each set. Also, a progressive loss of interest in the task might decrease the primacy effect. Finally, the subjects may simply become more skillful in handling the total communication as a single integrated unit, so that the primacy–recency distinction is less relevant. In any case, it is clear that it is not safe to generalize to situations involving many communications from the results of studies which employ only one or two communications.

Taken as a whole, the findings regarding primacy and recency (see also Lana, 1961) seem to rule out any universal principle of primacy in persuasion, but they have led to specifications of some of the sets of conditions which affect primacy. These factors include time of measurement, similarity of issues, contiguity of presentation, number of separate issues, earlier positive experiences with the communicator, interpolated activity, warnings against premature commitment, encouragement toward commitment, ambiguity inherent in the sequence of communications, and arousal of needs before proffering information. The effects of these factors are not due in any simple manner to learning or memory of evidence or arguments or to such factors as set, reinforcement, or attention. If anything, factors of acceptance may be the most critical. Thus, coming first makes a statement no more likely to be remembered, but does make it more likely to be believed; one side of an argument tends to be persuasive provided we have not heard the other side, and hearing one side after we have heard the other makes us more critical and skeptical.

As is true for the entire area of persuasive communication and attitude change, future study of the order of presentation should be based on the development of more elaborate theoretical models which take into account the laws of learning, perception, and motivation and on the conducting of crucial experiments which pit one theoretical approach against another. By invoking different theoretical formulations, we uncover sets of considerations which might never emerge as factors affecting the order of presentation if we relied on only one theoretical system.

Types of Appeal

In persuasive communications, what sorts of appeal operate most effectively in arousing motives to accept the opinions recommended? After reviewing numerous studies designed to provide answers to this question, Hovland, Janis, and Kelley (1953) conclude that the results have been inconsistent in showing, for instance, the superiority of "emotional" versus "rational" appeals, and that very few experimental studies have tested the effects of particular kinds of content in arousing particular kinds of motives. One reason for this paucity of data is the fact that it is often difficult in this kind of study to identify clearly the effective stimuli; there are few clear-cut criteria of, for instance, "emotional" or "rational" appeals. In addition, Hovland, Janis, and Kelley mention at least three aspects of audience responsiveness which might be differentially affected: (1) attention to the verbal content of the communication, (2) comprehension of the message of the communication, and (3) acceptance of the conclusions advocated by the communication (p. 59). Any one of these effects or any combination of them could account for the effectiveness of an appeal, so that it is necessary to distinguish these effects from each other for any systematic understanding of the way in which appeals intended to affect motivation might bring about change of attitude. However, earlier research on types of appeal has suggested a number of hypotheses for more rigorous investigation, in which different kinds of appeal may be introduced experimentally and the changes in attitude and behavior observed.

One such experimental study by Janis and Feshbach (1953) deals with the effects of a class of "emotional" appeals which we may refer to as "fear-arousing" or "threatening." The investigators began with the assumption that a threat is made when the contents of a communication allude to or describe unfavorable consequences that will allegedly result from a failure to adopt and adhere to the position advocated by the influencing agent. Appeals of this sort are regularly used in the everyday world, but what are the main factors that determine whether or not they will be successful? On the basis of general psychological theory, one may expect that a threatening appeal is most likely to induce an audience to accept the communicator's conclusion if (1) the emotional tension aroused during the communication is sufficiently intense to constitute a state of drive and (2) acceptance of the recommended attitude leads to the reduction of tension (Hovland *et al.,* 1953, pp. 61f.). Thus the most effective appeals are likely to be those which serve as reassurances, those that elicit anticipations of escaping from or averting the threat.

What factors, then, make for (1) the arousal of emotional tension and (2) after the arousal, the acceptance of the communicator's reassuring recommendation? The factors that influence arousal include the content of the appeal (the description of the dangers which will allegedly result from non-acceptance of the communicator's position; the nature of the evidence for the dangers), the source of the communication (the qualifications of the communicator—his expertness, credibility, and intentions), and the audience's antecedent experiences (prior "emotional inoculation," or preparation for and sensitization to the forthcoming appeal).

What of the second set of factors—the factors that, given the emotional tension, lead to acceptance of the communication and thereby to agreement with the communicator's position? One important requirement, as we have already seen (p. 12), is that presentation of the information which serves to alleviate emotional tension should immediately follow the arousal of that tension. Another factor is the degree to which acceptance of the position proposed will bring relief from danger. The most important factor, however, seems to be the degree to which defensive reactions occur when emotional tension is strongly aroused. These defensive reactions may militate against change of attitude by leading to distortion of the meaning of what is being said and by producing tendencies toward escape. The alleged dangers may thus be so horrible to contemplate that the audience, regardless of the evidence, refuses to consider them or to take them seriously.

In their experimental attack upon this problem, Janis and Feshbach presented college students with a fifteen-minute talk on dental hygiene. There were three different versions of the talk, each given to a different group of experimental subjects. Each talk contained essentially the same information about the causes of dental disease but differed in the amount of fear-arousing material. The first version (a strong fear-appeal) emphasized the painful consequences of tooth decay and its relation to cancer, blindness, and other ills. Slides illustrating diseased gums and other consequences of poor dental hygiene were shown. The second version (a moderate fear-appeal) presented these dangers in milder form, excluding the "facts" about cancer and blindness and making less of the painful consequences. The third version utilized a minimal fear-appeal containing more neutral material and fewer dire predictions.

The effects of the communications were measured by asking the subjects beforehand and afterward to describe the way they brushed their teeth, the kind of toothbrush they used, and other items of their dental practices (these topics were covered in the talks and certain recommendations about them were made to the subjects). Changes in these practices in the direction of acceptance of the offered recommendations were greatest in the group that received the communication containing the least fear-producing material. Another way of checking the effects consisted of re-exposing the audience to a second communication which discounted the recommendations of the first. Here also it was found that minimal fear-arousal was most effective: the audiences in the other groups were more inclined to accept the countercommunications which discounted the arguments in the original talk.

Thus the arousal of fear, if intense, may produce adverse effects. But why? First of all, strong emotions may cause inattentiveness to the communication because they increase distractibility and may temporarily impair cognitive functions.

Examination of the data from the preceding experiment showed that the efficiency of learning the factual material on dental hygiene was not observably reduced: the three forms of the communication were equally effective in teaching the factual material, as measured by an information test given immediately after exposure to the communication. An experiment by Janis and Milholland (1954) suggests, however, that there are some conditions under which "threat" appeals can exert an influence on what is learned and retained from a communication.

Aggressive feelings toward the communicator may modify the effects of strong fear-appeals. If the subjects feel that he is trying to frighten or frustrate them or has some particular manipulative intent, they may deliberately reject the conclusions as a way of expressing their aggression toward him. In general, the fear-appeals in the preceding experiment did not appear to evoke any large amount of aggression, and what there was of it was present in equal amounts under all three sets of conditions. Thus, while strong fear-appeals may sometimes produce hostility which would motivate rejection of the recommendations, that does not seem to have been a factor here.

A third factor in the present situation could have been defensive avoidance, occurring when an audience exposed to a strong threat is left in a state of emotional tension unrelieved by the reassurances in the communication. Janis and Feshbach incline toward this explanation; in write-in answers given by the subjects, fewer in the group that heard the strongest fear-appeal referred to the talk as authoritative and used its arguments. Thus when fear is strongly aroused but is not adequately relieved by the reassurances in the communication, the subject is motivated to ignore or minimize the importance of the threat.

This generalization about the effects of fear-appeals, insofar as it was inferred from findings based on measures of the effectiveness of communications obtained by comparing responses to questionnaires before and after communication, had until recently merely the status of a reasonable though far from conclusive hypothesis. A new study by Janis and Terwilliger (1962), however, obtained direct measures of the resistances that tend to be mobilized by a strong fear-appeal during exposure to a communication. Although the results are not un-equivocal, the study provides the most direct support yet obtained for the general notion that when a relatively high level of fear is induced by the warnings presented in a persuasive communication, the recipients will tend to develop psychological resistances to the communicator's arguments, conclusions, and recommendations.

An experiment by Goldstein (1959) explicitly investigates some of the personality dynamics assumed by Janis and Feshbach to underlie the effectiveness of fear-arousing propaganda. In this experiment the responses of "copers" and "avoiders" to fear-arousing communications were compared. Copers handle threatening stimulation directly by problem-solving; avoiders try to bypass and put aside the intrusion of threatening material. Previous research had suggested that in a sentence-completion task, copers excel in recall for disturbing material, whereas avoiders are better at recalling neutral material. Thus it was hypothesized that the acceptance of the recommendations contained in a strong fear-appeal would be greater for the copers, but that when the material was presented in a relatively neutral context, as in a minimal fear-appeal, it should gain greater acceptance among the avoiders.

Here too dental hygiene served as the issue in the high-fear-inducing and low-fear-inducing talks. After the talks, subjects in each group answered questionnaires designed to show dental practices, to provide dental information, and to induce anxiety about diseases of the gums and mouth. The results support the hypothesis that a strong fear-appeal receives greater acceptance among copers than among avoiders. The effect, however, appears to be due to the differential effectiveness of the appeals on the avoiders (that is to say the low-fear condition was more effective for them), whereas the copers reacted similarly to both sets of conditions. Thus the copers—possibly because of their ability to deal with emotional stimuli—were apparently not more affected by the strong appeal to fear; if they were at all willing to change their habits because of perceived danger, they were just as apt to do so when the danger was relatively slight as when it was relatively great.

This experiment broadens somewhat the base of the research on types of appeal. While it indicates that fear-appeals may operate through the kinds of psychodynamics mentioned by Janis and Feshbach, it suggests further that the specification of factors mediating between fear-appeals and their acceptance is by no means a simple task.

Weiss and Fine (1956) investigated another type of emotional appeal by using a communication with an aggressive or punitive orientation. The investigators' hypothesis was that persons aroused to aggressiveness would be more influenced by a communication which was punitively oriented and less influenced by one oriented toward leniency than persons who were not aggressively aroused. This experiment again attempts to link the motives or needs aroused by a communication with its recommendations or appeals: a communication's effectiveness is facilitated if some congruency exists between the predispositions of the audience and the appeals made in the communication. In order to test this assumption, the investigators first measured attitudes on two interesting topics—juvenile delinquency and America's relations with her allies. Then one group of subjects was exposed to a failure-insult procedure: they were given designs of great complexity to work on as part of a problem-solving task, were made to fail a very high proportion of the trials, and were subjected to uncomplimentary and insulting comments about their performance, insults which increased in intensity over the trials. The other half of the subjects were placed in an ego-satisfying situation where they experienced success and had complimentary and encouraging remarks made to them. Under an irrelevant pretext, both groups were then asked to read articles on juvenile delinquency or on America's diplomatic relations, articles which were structured in terms of either lenient attitudes or punitive responses toward delinquents or foreign countries. Finally, the subjects were given a number of postexperimental measures, among which were the items about juvenile delinquency and America's allies as given before the session. Changes in these two sets of measures, from before to after the aggressive or ego-satisfying arousal, constitute the main data of this experiment.

The data support the hypothesis that aggressively aroused

subjects will be more influenced by a punitively oriented communication and less influenced by a leniently oriented communication than will nonaggressive subjects. As the authors interpret the results, the experience of failure, accompanied by insults, aroused aggression which could not be expressed against the higher status of the experimenter. Thus acceptance of the punitively oriented communication may function as an outlet for the subjects' feelings of aggressiveness. The authors conclude that the arousal of aggression predisposes a person to certain changes of opinion, but for the predisposition to be effective, specific appeals coordinate with the arousal must be used. It should be noted, however, that variables of personality are important factors in the effectiveness of appeals that arouse needs; in Weiss and Fine's experiment, the individual's characteristic predispositions toward aggression as well as how he expresses aggression are likely to be important determinants of how he is affected by fear-arousing appeals. Evidence on this issue is relevant to the role that personality variations play in attitude change (see Ch. 4).

While experiments have thus thrown some light on the conditions under which emotional appeals may be more or less effective in producing attitude changes in their recipients, other research (including Lewan & Stotland, 1961; Weiss & Lieberman, 1959) suggests that a great deal of work remains to be done before we arrive at a systematic grasp of the issue. For one thing, the theoretical models which have been invoked to explain the effects of types of appeal have by and large had to do only with negative feelings and have not usually dealt with those emotional appeals which arouse sympathy, affection, elation, satisfaction, or other "positive" emotions. While the threatening communication may have many implications for other types of propaganda, a question remains for research as to whether there may not be unique effects of pleas which appeal to the positive, moral, ethical, and even the religious sides of people. This issue is but one of many awaiting clarification through systematic, controlled experimental research.

2

CHARACTERISTICS OF THE COMMUNICATOR

WHO SAYS something is as important as *what* is said in understanding the effect of a communication on an attitude. How the listener perceives the communicator can affect attitude change in numerous ways: the vividness of his personality, his status, the expertise attributed to him, the stake he has in the issue— all of these may make a difference. Many attitudes can underlie the effects: affection and admiration for the communicator, fear and awe of him, trust and confidence in his sincerity, fairness, and credibility.

The Credibility of the Communicator

Most of the research on the role of the characteristics of the communicator has centered on situations in which the effects are attributable to one clear-cut source, the communicator, and in which the major characteristic investigated has been the communicator's credibility. Hovland and Weiss (1951) gave college students identical communications to read; these were represented as excerpts from newspaper and magazine articles.

The articles dealt with such topics as the feasibility of an atomic submarine, antihistamine drugs, the steel situation, and the future of movie theaters. In half of the presentations, the communications were attributed to sources found on an earlier questionnaire to be considered trustworthy (statements about the atomic submarine were attributed to a famous American nuclear physicist), and in the other half to such untrustworthy sources as *Pravda*. The subjects were given questionnaires both before and after presentation of the material; they were also asked to rate the fairness and justifiability of the presentation. The investigators also measured the amount of information the subjects retained.

Although the subjects acquired the same amounts of information under all sets of conditions, they judged identical presentations as less fair and the conclusions as less justified when the communications were attributed to sources of low rather than high credibility. Change of attitude in the direction advocated by the communication was greater when it originated from the highly credible source than when it came from the low one. It is important to note, however, that the change was observed *immediately* after the presentation.

Kelman and Hovland (1953) asked high school students to listen to a recording of an educational program in which a speaker advocated extreme leniency in the treatment of juvenile delinquency. Three variations of the credibility of the source were given to different groups of students. In the "positive" version, the speaker was described as a judge in a juvenile court, highly trained, well-informed, authoritative, sincere, honest, and with the public interest at heart. In the "neutral" version, the speaker was identified as a member of the studio audience who had been chosen at random; no information about him was given. In the "negative" condition, he was also presented as selected from the studio audience, but it became clear in the introduction that he had been a delinquent in his youth, was involved in some shady deals at the moment, and was out on bail on a charge of drug-peddling.

A questionnaire on attitudes toward the treatment of criminals was administered immediately after the presentation of the communication. There was no prior measure of attitude, but since the subjects were randomly assigned to the three conditions, the three groups may be taken as initially comparable. As we should expect, the negative source was judged to be less fair and trustworthy than the positive source, with the neutral source falling in between. The data on attitude are consistent with the perceptions of the source: the group hearing the communication from the positive source favored more lenient treatment than those hearing it from the negative source. The neutral group was close to the positive group in their attitudes toward leniency. The characterization of the communicator as biased had little effect on the learning of the content of the communication, but it did influence the degree to which it was accepted.

Hovland and Mandell's study (1952) also provides data relevant to the issue of the communicator's trustworthiness. Within the framework of their tests of the effects of drawing conclusions, where the statement of principles and examples led to a conclusion favoring the recommendation of the communicator (see p. 6), they used an introduction that elicited suspicion of the communicator's motives with half of the subjects, and with the other half one that evoked belief in his impartiality. In effect, the first group was expected to infer that the communicator had something to gain from pushing his point and having it accepted, whereas to the other group he was introduced as an economist from a leading American university. The subjects gave their opinions before and after the speech and also gave their reactions to the program and speaker. The results show that, though the contents of the speeches and the conclusions were identical, the "motivated" speaker was rated as less fair and honest and as having given a poorer presentation than the "impartial" speaker. There appeared to be no differences, however, between the groups in their amounts of attitude change.

Two more recent experiments also bear, though indirectly, on the question of the communicator's characteristics. In the first (Walster & Festinger, 1962), communications on highly salient issues were found to produce more attitude change when they were "accidentally overheard" by subjects than when the subjects knew the communications were intended to influence them. In the second (Festinger & Maccoby, 1964), a persuasive communication arguing against fraternities was more effective in changing attitudes when it was accompanied by an irrelevant film about abstract painting than when it was played as the sound track of an anti-fraternity film. Both experiments may be broadly interpreted as reflecting the increased attitude change which comes about when there is a reduced imputation to the agent of persuasion of an intent to influence. The "accidental" character of the communication in the first case, and the fact that the irrelevant stimulus in the second may have led to some distraction, presumably caused subjects to be less motivated to erect defenses against the communicator and the communication and therefore to be more influenced by them.

In evaluating the results of all these studies, a special caution must be introduced. The effect of a speaker's credibility, his trustworthiness and impartiality, is not a simple one but depends to some degree on other conditions. Variations in other factors may produce one situation in which the perceived impartiality of the communicator makes a difference and another in which it does not. While judgment of credibility and change of attitude went hand in hand in the experiments of Hovland and Weiss (1951) and Kelman and Hovland (1953), the fact that they were not supported in the studies of Hovland and Mandell (1952) and Weiss (1961) suggests that further research is needed in order to determine the conditions under which this outcome will or will not occur. One persistent theoretical problem is that of disentangling the main components of credibility. Is it expertness or trustworthiness, perception of fairness or bias, disinterest or propagandistic intent, or any combination of these factors which is responsible for the effects of credibility on attitude change?

Some light is shed on this question when we refer back to Kelman and Hovland's experiment (see pp. 24-25). It will be recalled that the reactions of the group which heard the neutral source were more like those of the positive group than those of the negative group. This result suggested to Hovland, Janis, and Kelley (1953) that attitudes toward the fairness and trustworthiness of the source played a greater role than attitudes toward expertness in leading to attitude change in the direction advocated.

Evidence from the study by Weiss and Fine (1956) bears on this issue. Their data suggest, however, that judgment of fairness is more closely related to the effectiveness of a communication in producing change of attitude than is judgment of propagandistic intent. All communicators may be seen as having an axe to grind (Weiss, 1957), so that propagandistic intent may not in itself be particularly important with regard to the persuasiveness of a communication. If the propagandistic effect is perceived as unfair, however, the resulting increases in counteracting responses and the decrement in attention and acceptance may lead to less attitude change. It may well be that the most potent aspect of credibility is the perceived fairness of presentation; perception of motivation to persuade may by itself be relatively less important in predicting the effectiveness of a persuasive communication. These suggestions have many implications for understanding the determinants of a communication's effectiveness, but a good deal more research must be done before we can adequately separate out the different factors in the credibility of communicators.

A number of recent experiments help clarify the dimensions of credibility and their effectiveness in determining attitude change. For example, a study by Weiss (1957) was concerned with whether a statement by a communicator which agrees with the views of an audience on one important issue will affect the communicator's real purpose of changing the audience's opinions on another, unrelated issue. In other words, if the source is trustworthy, does his siding with the audience on one issue lead to greater acceptance of his views on another issue? Weiss's results imply that it does, though the psychological processes underlying the effect are not entirely clear. The effect may operate through an enhancement of the trustworthiness of the communicator either by emphasizing that he is a man of sound judgment or by emphasizing his oneness with the audience. In either case, the effect may be to disarm the audience.

Allyn and Festinger (1961) made a study in which a communicator recommended to an audience of teen-agers that the minimum age for driving an automobile be raised. We should expect, of course, that such a position would initially have been opposed by teen-agers but that pressures toward change of attitude would be in the direction of accepting the communicator's message. Before hearing the persuasive message, however, half of the subjects were told that the purpose of the program was to study the personality of the speaker, whereas the other half were told that the speaker considered teen-agers a menace on the roads. Thus differential perceptions of the communicator's motives and biases were introduced: in the first group, the subjects' attention was directed away from the speaker's intent to persuade; in the second, the group-identity of the members of the audience, the hostility of the speaker to the group, and his manifest intent to persuade were all emphasized. Both two weeks before and immediately after the communication, the subjects filled out a questionnaire that included four items on the issue of teen-age driving. It would be expected that the second group of subjects would perceive the communicator as more biased. The data show that the second group of subjects did indeed see the communicator as more biased and that the first group showed greater change toward the position advocated.

Weiss and Fine (1955) found that those subjects who viewed a communication calling for harsh treatment and strict discipline for juvenile delinquents as fair and not propagandistic were affected more than those who found it unfair and loaded with propaganda and also changed their attitudes more into line with the message of the communication.

Finally, an experiment by Aronson and Golden (1962) indicates that not only are variables which are fully relevant to the content of the persuasive communication and which are also of general relevance (intelligence, honesty, sincerity, responsibility) important in affecting attitude change, but that those positive and negative aspects of a communicator that bear no objective relevance to the topic of communication are also important. Both relevant and irrelevant aspects of credibility determine change of attitude; audiences are not composed of people who respond only to the objectively relevant aspects of a communicator. Thus, for example, whether a person is effective may depend on whether he is perceived as an expert, but also on whether he is fat, sloppy, neat, ugly, handsome, a poor athlete, or a member of a minority group. This generalization reflects people's tendencies to make use of all the information they possess about a social situation in forming a general impression on which they can act. One trait or characteristic influences another, and they all combine to produce a general effect on change of attitude. A more extensive discussion of the ways in which diverse cognitions are organized and affect attitude is presented in Chapter 5.

The data from these different experiments show with reasonably good agreement that variations in the credibility of the communicator do indeed determine variations in attitude change: the greater the trustworthiness or expertness, the greater the change toward the position advocated by the communicator. While differences in the credibility of the source seem not to affect the learning of the content of a communication, they do appear to affect its acceptance. Hovland, Janis, and Kelley (1953) assume that this result comes about because the individual is motivated to accept conclusions and recommendations which he anticipates will lead to social approval or to avoidance of punishment. Anticipation of these states is increased when the communication is presented by a person who is respected, informed, insightful, and sincere and decreased when there are cues of low credibility. Yet, as noted earlier, the lack of complete uniformity among the findings necessitates a better specification of the situations in which such motivation is stronger or weaker. One such condition may apply in situations in which fine discriminations are required: specialized information and expertness not available to the individual may increase his motivation to seek and accept advice from credible sources.

The Amount of Change Advocated

An interesting issue concerns the amount of change of opinion advocated by the communicator. Hovland (1959) makes the following generalizations based on a review of relevant research: under conditions where there is some ambiguity about the credibility of the communicator, the greater the attempt at change, the higher the resistance; but with respected communicators, the greater the discrepancy between the subject's position and the one advocated, the greater the change. Although the subject's involvement with the issue may be an important factor here, there is some evidence that Hovland's generalization is valid. In experiments by Hovland, Harvey, and Sherif (1957) and Fisher and Lubin (1958), the ambiguity of the source's credibility may have led to greater resistance when advocacy was greater; in experiments by Hovland and Pritzker (1957), Goldberg (1954), and Zimbardo (1960), the use of a highly credible source led to greater change when there was greater discrepancy between communicator and subject. Zimbardo's experiment will serve to illustrate the effects of a positive source.

Zimbardo's design provided for experimental variation of the discrepancy between the communicator's and the subject's position. The communicator was a source of high credibility. College girls serving as subjects were asked to bring a close friend into the laboratory with them. These pairs were then led to believe that they had disagreed either a little or a lot with regard to judgments of a case study of juvenile delinquency. Since the pairs of girls were close friends who had chosen to come to the session together, we may assume that each constituted a source of high credibility for the other. The reception of another's judgment and the fact that it is discrepant from one's own sets up pressures to change judgment in the direction of the friend's. Zimbardo found that the greater the distance between friends in their judgments, the more they changed their attitudes in the direction expected.

The studies mentioned above and the Zimbardo study do not deal, however, with what would happen if a negative communicator were the source of the message. In the Hovland, Harvey, and Sherif (1957) experiment, there was an assumption that the source was ambiguous, but it was not clear that it was explicitly negative, and in the Hovland and Pritzker (1957), Goldberg (1954), and Zimbardo (1960) studies only a positive communicator was used, with no variation in which there was a negative communicator. To assess the validity of Hovland's generalization we need an experiment where both positive and negative sources are used in the same situation. If highly positive sources lead to a direct relationship between discrepancy and change and less positive or negative sources lead to an inverse relationship in an experiment where the same setting and materials are used, we can have greater confidence in the generalization.

Such an experiment was carried out by Aronson, Turner, and Carlsmith (1963). In their experiment, subjects were exposed to a communication which was identical for all groups except for variation in the credibility of the communicator and in the discrepancy between the advocated opinion and the subjects' position. The subjects were college girls who were asked to rank-order stanzas from obscure modern poems under the guise of an experiment in esthetics. They ranked these stanzas on the basis of an ambiguous criterion of "use of form to express meaning." Then each subject read a communication about modern poetry which contained recommendations about the particular stanza which she had initially ranked eighth. For one third of the subjects, there was a small discrepancy between her opinion of the stanza and the communicator's opinion, for one third a moderate discrepancy, for the last third an extreme discrepancy. Half of each of these groups was given a communication purported to be from a highly credible source (T. S. Eliot); the other half received a communication supposedly from a mildly credible source (a student). The subjects re-ranked the stanzas immediately afterward. Since a subject's original ranking of the particular stanza was known, the change in her ranking of the stanza could be determined as a function of discrepancy and credibility.

Subjects who read the communication from the highly credible source showed greater change of opinion when the opinion of the source was presented as more discrepant from their own. For the less credible source, increasing the discrepancy led to greater change of opinion up to a certain point, but, as the discrepancy became more extreme, the degree of change decreased. Thus, in experimental situations where there is no possibility of changing the communicator's opinion but when he can be disparaged as a source (as under conditions of lower credibility), the subject does so; and the greater the difference from the subject's own position, the greater the disparagement and the less the resulting change of opinion. A highly credible source cannot easily be disparaged, however, and the difference in opinion between the subject and the highly credible communicator, which may be disturbing to the subject, can be reduced by the subject's changing toward the communicator; the greater the change advocated, the greater the resulting change.

An experiment by Bergin (1962) provides further confirmation of this line of reasoning. Communicators of varying credibility gave persuasive communications about subjects' personalities, accounts which varied in their degree of discrepancy from the subjects' initial ideas about themselves. The data show again that amount of change on the part of the subjects toward accepting the communicator's view of them increased as a direct function of degree of discrepancy under high-credibility conditions, in contrast to little or no change under conditions where the communicator was of low credibility.

The Persistence of Change

A final question bearing on credibility concerns the durability of the effects. In terms of immediate effects, the highly credible sources seem to be more effective in bringing about change than sources of lower credibility. But what happens to these effects over time? Evidence from delayed aftertests, as in the experiments by Hovland and Weiss (1951) and Kelman and Hovland (1953) indicates that the advantage of high over low credibility disappears after an interval of about three weeks.

In the Hovland and Weiss experiment, for instance, the effects were tested by measurement of the influence of credibility four weeks later as well as immediately afterward. After four weeks, the amount of opinion change for the two credibility groups was equal: about at the point initially obtained for the negative source and below that obtained for the positive source.

A clue to the nature of the process underlying the diminishing advantage of highly credible sources over time is provided by a phenomenon first noticed by Hovland, Lumsdaine, and Sheffield (1949) in one of their Army studies. They found that, while memory of factual material conveyed by a film had shown a decrease with time, changes of opinion increased on some items of opinion. They called this phenomenon a "sleeper effect" and suggested the following explanation. Suppose that the film has two immediate effects: (1) It conveys certain information favorable to a particular attitude, and (2) It arouses reactions of skepticism and resistance to the attempt at influence. From the point of view of attitude change, the second effect damps the first. But suppose that the second effect wears off—is forgotten—faster than the first. Then subjects would go on remembering the information relevant to attitude but would lose track of whatever it was that evoked their skepticism and resistance. The net effect would be precisely what was observed. Hovland, Janis, and Kelley (1953) advance a similar explanation for the diminishing effect of the communicator's credibility over time. When the source is one of high credibility, there are initially two effects: (1) the information effect and (2) the source effect, which enhances the listener's desire to agree or diminishes his desire to examine the information critically. When the source is one of low credibility, there are again the same two kinds of effect, except that the second takes the form of increasing the listener's resistance and critical reaction to the information. If the recollection of the source tends to disappear while much of the information is retained, the subject reacts to the information with his normal (uninfluenced) critical assessment of information. The information from the highly credible source thus loses its advantage, whereas the less credible source loses its disadvantage. If the information itself is moderately compelling toward attitude change, but not perfectly so, the net source-versus-information effect will diminish in the case of high credibility and increase in the case of low credibility until only the information itself remains effective; and if the information itself is gradually forgotten, the effect of the attempt at influence will, from that point on, go on diminishing equally in both groups.

In other words, the loss in the effects of prestige over time may be due to dissociation of source from content. With the passage of time, the content of a statement is less likely to be spontaneously associated with the source; people often remember what was said without thinking about who said it.

A further caution concerning sleeper effects is also in order. Festinger (1955) has called attention to the lack of control over the interaction among subjects in these experiments. He notes that the use of large classes of students as experimental subjects has often led experimenters to divide each class so that a number of different experimental conditions were used in the same class. During the time that elapsed between the immediate and the delayed testing there could have been a good deal of interaction among members of the class, so that those who had received the untrustworthy communication talked with those who had received the trustworthy one, and vice versa. The subjects could have discussed the issues on which their opinions had been measured, and thus the differences between them which the well-balanced design had created would lead to an influence process which would move them back toward agreement. The sleeper effect might then be attributable simply to the operation of social influence among the subjects. The fact that reminding them of the original source re-creates the difference does not resolve the ambiguity of the interpretation of the sleeper effect. This problem of interaction within a class where different experimental conditions are replicated and a delayed measurement is made can be overcome by using a separate class for each set of experimental conditions. Nevertheless, this procedure too has its disadvantages. Unless many classes are used for each condition, idiosyncratic class norms may lead to an artificial result where the effects can be attributed to the particular characteristics of a specific class. In any event, while we do not have to assess the validity of Festinger's criticism with regard to the present discussion, we must be alive to the pervasive importance of the phenomena of group interaction if we are to obtain a rounded picture of the determinants of attitude change and social influence. We shall go into these problems in greater detail in Chapter 7.

The sleeper effect was directly tested in the experiment by Kelman and Hovland (1953). In their experiment, it will be recalled, positive, negative, and neutral communicators gave speeches on juvenile delinquency. At the time of the delayed testing of opinion, the source was "reinstated" for half the subjects by replaying the introduction to the communication that the subjects had heard three weeks earlier. In the situation where there was no reinstatement of the source, the change of opinion from the time of initial testing to the test given three weeks later was the same for the positive and negative conditions, a result consistent with that obtained by Hovland and Weiss (the sleeper effect). Under conditions of reinstatement, however, the change was higher for the positive communicator and lower for the negative communicator.

The effects we have been discussing are complex, and it is obvious that they may be so much more complex that any simply stated generalization is suspect. Thus, a subject may forget the sources of some information while retaining the information; but he may remember the source and change in his attitude toward the source. On the kind of reasoning we have reviewed, this, too, should have consequences. Similarly, on the information side, there is not merely the substantive content of the message, but there are also cues as to how strongly the source feels about the issue. Suppose that his perception of the issue changes with time. Should not this change also have some consequence? Or suppose that the message has asserted that certain statements are true and others false and that the subject remembers the statements but cannot recall (or misremembers) which were said to be true and which false—or, further, that he remembers more of the "false" statements than of the "true" while forgetting that they were labeled false. Moreover, the information that he acquires may include information about the reactions of the audience, and, if this has consequences, changes associated with the retention or forgetting of this information (or in his relation to the members of the audience) should also have consequences. In brief, if we have learned anything in this chapter, it is not the universal validity of any propositions concerning the effects of characteristics of the communicator or such phenomena as sleeper effects; what we have learned is to become sensitive to certain kinds of psychological process.

3

APPROVAL AND DISAPPROVAL

HOVLAND, Janis, and Kelley (1953), in discussing the effects of the communicator's credibility, mention various expectations that affect a person's motivation to accept or reject a communication. These expectations include being right or wrong, being impartially advised or being manipulated by the communicator, and being approved of or disapproved of by others, especially by authoritative communicators. As the investigators say, "It seems likely that such expectations are capable of arousing strong motives which have been acquired on the basis of prior experiences in which the individual has been rewarded (correctly advised, benefited, and socially approved) or punished (misled, exploited, and socially disapproved) as a consequence of believing and accepting what other people have told him" (p. 292).

The expectation of disapproval or approval has been considered a major incentive in persuasion. A prestigious communicator is often perceived as a barometer of the social climate of any social situation and as someone whose approval or disapproval is very important. On the other hand, the desire for approval from a reference group opposed to the communicator tends to facilitate rejection of a persuasive communication. Social learning has ensured that we attend to the words of prestigeful persons because their approval has consequences for other rewards and punishments. It has also led to our concern over the reactions of our peers and of members of other social groups to which we belong, since they too can dispense social rewards and punishments. Let us examine some findings relevant to the implications for attitude change of expectations of reward or punishment, as dispensed both by prestigious communicators and by others around us.

Studies of the Effects of Approval and Disapproval

A number of studies have investigated directly the effects of giving approval or disapproval in inducing attitude change. Singer (1961) found that the experimenter's saying "good" or "right," depending upon whether the subject agreed or disagreed with statements reflecting authoritarian attitudes, was effective in shifting subjects to a different position on a scale of attitude designed to measure those authoritarian attitudes. When "good" or "right" was given each time subjects agreed with democratic and antiauthoritarian attitudes, they showed change toward a more "democratic" position.

Hildum and Brown (1956) studied the effects of approval in the course of a survey of attitudes about general education. When asked later about their opinions, those to whom the experimenter had responded "good" had changed their attitudes in a manner consistent with the reinforcement more than those to whom the experimenter had merely said "mm-hmm."

A series of more elaborate studies was carried out by Scott. In his first study (Scott, 1957) he induced college students to engage in debates on three different issues: Universal Military Training, night hours for women students, and deemphasis of football. Before the debates, however, he had administered questionnaires measuring the students' attitudes toward these issues. In their debates, the subjects took sides opposite those they had indicated as their own in the pretest. After the "debate," half of the subjects were rewarded for verbalizing their position by being told that they were "winners"; the other half were told that they were "losers." These convictions were produced by arranging a false vote on the part of the class before whom the "debates" took place. The results of the experiment showed that the subjects who were told that they were winners showed significantly greater change of attitude toward the position they were upholding than did the subjects who were told that they were losers.

In a second experiment, Scott (1959a) used a somewhat different procedure. In the presence of three judges, the subject was asked first to present the side of the issue he was to uphold (opposite to his own position); a confederate of the experimenter then supported the subject's side and the subject was given an opportunity to reply. During the discussion, the judges showed sympathetic interest in what the subject said and afterward they thanked the participants for their "interesting ideas." A final measure of attitude indicated that subjects whose verbal behavior was praised changed their attitudes toward the position they had presented.

A later experiment by Scott (1959b) showed that subjects who debated an issue and were reinforced by a vote of their classmates (they were voted "winners") changed their attitudes more toward the position they upheld than did "losers," regardless of whether they debated their own side of the argument, advocated the opposite side, or started from an initially neutral position. The results indicated that the change had some degree of permanence, since it was evident on a second posttest taken a week after the debate.

Group Membership and Attitude Change

An important source of social approval and disapproval, the expectation of which affects attitude change, is the social group to which a person belongs. Many research findings which show that members of a group resist communications that run counter to the norms and values of the group and accept those sanctioned by it can be interpreted in terms of expectations of social approval or disapproval. An example of the influence of one's peers on attitude change and development is presented by an experiment by Rhine (1958). In this experiment, some subjects made responses after hearing the responses of three confederates who were supposed to be fellow students, whereas other subjects made their responses in private. The results showed that the subjects who heard the confederates' responses adopted a similar attitude more readily than those who responded in private.

Kelley and Woodruff (1956) investigated what happens if members of a group who are listening to a persuasive communication which is contrary to their group norms learn that other members have expressed approval of the communication. In this experiment, a group of students at a progressively oriented teachers' college listened to a recorded speech which called for a return to more traditional classroom methods than those advocated by so-called progressive educators. The major argument was that recent research on learning and motivation had cast doubt on many modern teaching procedures and that the schools should insist on greater respect for authority, on the fulfillment of standard requirements, and on the acquisition of basic knowledge and skills. Seven times during the speech applause was interpolated, apparently made by the audience present at the time the speech was recorded. The manipulation of approval or sanction from one's own group was accomplished by identifying the supposed applauding audience differently. Half of the subjects were told that they were listening to "members' applause"—that is, that prestigeful members of their college group made up the audience; the other half were told that "outsiders" constituted the audience. Those who were exposed to the members' applause exhibited more immediate change in the direction of the persuasive speech than did those who were told it was outsiders' applause. Thus, the experimenters conclude, change in group-anchored opinions can be facilitated by conveying information that other group members have changed their opinions.

Kelley and Volkhart (1952) found that persons who are

most strongly motivated to retain their membership in a group and therefore depend most upon approval from the group are less likely to accept communications which advocate positions counter to the norms and values of the group. The subjects of this study were Boy Scouts, who were measured on their attitudes toward camping and woodcraft and also on their valuation of their membership in the troop. When an outside adult later criticized the Scouts' emphasis on camping and woodcraft, those who valued their membership least changed their attitudes toward these activities most toward conformity with the adult's attitude. This relationship between valuation of membership and resistance to attitude change was even more striking when the subjects' attitudes were measured anonymously, an illustration of the fact that approval or disapproval does not actually have to be received to be effective. What often seems to matter most is that one should have earned the approval and not merited the disapproval of the group.

These experiments support the proposition that expectations of social approval or disapproval play an important role in whether or not persons will change their attitudes in response either to a persuasive communication or to the simple expression of a point of view by someone else, whether he be an authoritative experimenter or a peer. Those who place a high value on their membership in a group are most vulnerable to threats of social punishment from the group, inasmuch as they have the strongest motives to maintain friendly relationships with fellow members and the strongest desire to secure the prestige and privileges associated with their status as members. Their attitudes therefore tend to change more, or less, in one direction or another depending upon the relation of the change to the group's standards. We shall return to the effects of group membership on attitude change in Chapter 7.

4

PERSONALITY PREDISPOSITIONS AND PERSUASIVE COMMUNICATIONS

THE PRECEDING chapters have dealt with characteristics of the communication and of the communicator. The present chapter turns to the question of audience predispositions and focuses on certain of the manifold connections between a persuasive communication and the personality of the individual toward whom it is directed. Some of the questions to be considered are: What determines a person's readiness to accept or reject a point of view that is being urged on him? Are some people more susceptible in general to persuasive communications than others, and what determines their susceptibility or lack of it?

Each of three areas of research makes somewhat different assumptions about the connection between personality and attitude change. The first area concerns general persuasibility. Is there a general trait of persuasibility which promotes acceptance of persuasive communications no matter what the topic or issue? The second area concerns differential susceptibility to various kinds of communication, but again the variation is unrelated to the specific topics; it involves such matters as the clarity or ambiguity of the communication and the significance of personal styles of processing information. The third area introduces the tailoring of issues of specific content to the arousal of specific psychodynamic processes. Thus the following discussion will move from a topic-free model of analysis to another model which is also topic-free but which makes assumptions about the way the message is organized and the kinds of people who receive it and then to a third which is topic-bound in the sense that specific personality predispositions are assumed to have implications for specific kinds of attitude.

Personality and Persuasibility

In their 1953 volume, *Communication and Persuasion,* Hovland, Janis, and Kelley, after looking at the evidence then extant on the relationship between personality and susceptibility to persuasion, conclude that people may show "fairly consistent tendencies to be highly influenced or to remain uninfluenced by each of a series of discrete topics on different communications." They express the hope that "a number of more or less general factors will eventually be isolated, some of which may apply to a broad range of communications situations" (pp. 178f.). They go on to designate persuasibility *as a generic term which refers to any general tendency to respond positively, regardless of how such a tendency may have arisen.*

The hope expressed by Hovland, Janis, and Kelley stimulated further research, and their one chapter on this topic grew into a book of contributions by different investigators, edited by Hovland and Janis and published in 1959 under the title *Personality and Persuasibility.* A brief summary of some of the main points of this volume will provide an overview of the knowledge that has accumulated on the relationships between personality predispositions and the general trait of persuasibility.

Consistency of Individual Differences

The editors of *Personality and Persuasibility,* after presenting a series of relevant experimental studies, conclude that there is evidence of a trait of persuasibility which is independent of the subject matter or kinds of appeal presented in a given persuasive communication. The evidence comes from three different studies. The first, by Janis and Field, set up a procedure whereby subjects were persuaded first in one direction and then in another on the same set of issues, although the persuasive communications used to sway them varied in type of appeal and arguments. In order for a change of opinion to be counted as such, a subject who had changed in one direction in response to the first set of communications had to change back in response to the second set of communications. This procedure was repeated for each subject with a variety of communications. Statistical analysis of the intercorrelations between persuasibility subscores on each communication supported the hypothesis.

Another study, by King, showed that as a result of the influence of majority opinion, some high school students changed their positions on many different topics more than others. This difference in susceptibility to persuasion occurred with different sources of majority opinion (parents, other high school students, high school teachers).

A third study, by Abelson and Lesser, used three tests of general persuasibility with children as subjects. In the first, a communicator (either a teacher or an experimenter) showed a pair of pictures of objects and then indicated her own preference before asking the subject to state his. The second was a test using incomplete stories, each of which presented a parental figure stating a novel opinion or bit' of advice; the subject was asked to tell what the child in the story would do or think in response. In the third, the subjects listened to a tape recording which posed unusual questions about opinions; then, before giving their views, they heard another recording on which adult voices or peer voices expressed opinions unanimously in favor of one side of an issue. Intercorrelations between the measures on the three tests again supported the hypothesis of a trait of general persuasibility.

Sources of Persuasibility: Self-Esteem

In another chapter in the same book, Janis and Field show that high persuasibility appears to be related to low self-esteem as measured by feelings of inadequacy, social inhibitions, and test anxiety. An experiment by Janis and Rife investigated these relationships in institutionalized mental patients. Their confirmatory and even stronger findings suggest that the personality predispositions which are assumed to underlie persuasibility in the population at large are more pronounced in emotionally disturbed persons than Janis and Field had found to be the case for normal persons.

A somewhat different approach defines self-esteem as the value an individual places on himself (Cohen, 1959a). It is assumed to be a function of past success and failure in meeting aspirations, in other words a function of the discrepancy between a person's ideals and his achievement of them. After sorting subjects into categories of high and low self-esteem, Cohen found that persons of low self-esteem tended to be more susceptible to influence from persons of higher self-esteem than vice versa and to be less active in attempting to exert influence. Insofar as attempts at persuasion generally come from seemingly self-assured sources, this finding is consistent with the notion that persons of low self-esteem are generally susceptible to persuasive influence.

This line of research further attempts to link self-esteem and, by inference, susceptibility to attitude change with personality dynamics, emotional conflicts, ego-defenses, and similar concepts growing out of psychoanalytic theory. Employing the concept of ego-defense against underlying psychosexual conflicts, Cohen isolated and measured by projective tests two groups of defenses, the avoidance defenses (reaction formation, repression, and denial) and expressive defenses (projection and regression). He suggests that persons of low self-esteem are characterized by expressive defenses which sensitize them to environmental stimuli and make them vulnerable to the influence of external events, whereas persons of high self-esteem who use avoidance defenses are able to repress, deny, or ignore challenging experiences stemming from the environment and to maintain a stable self-picture at a high level. On the basis of this view of self-esteem, Cohen hypothesized that threatening appeals are more likely to be rejected by those of high self-esteem than by those of low self-esteem. On the other hand, appeals which enhance an individual's self-picture may be accepted more readily by the highs than by the lows.

A recent experiment (Leventhal & Perloe, 1962) confirmed Cohen's hypothesis with a group of college undergraduates who were measured on their attitudes toward Army life before and after they were given persuasive communications. Half of the subjects received communications which were optimistic and buoyant about Army life and half received communications which were negativistic, pessimistic, and hostile. The results showed that the subjects with high self-esteem, assumed to be avoidance-oriented, were more readily influenced by the optimistic, gratifying, potentially self-enhancing communications than by the pessimistic, threatening ones. Subjects with low self-esteem, who were expected to use expressive or sensitizing defenses, showed the opposite effect. Thus, the specification of self-esteem and its underlying psychosexual components permits an isolation of some critical variables which can account for differences in the acceptance of persuasive communications.

A number of other personality factors have been suggested as affecting persuasibility (Hovland & Janis, 1959):

1. *Perceptual dependence.* Subjects whose perceptions of physical stimuli are affected by the surrounding environmental field are more susceptible to persuasive communications than those who rely on their own bodily experiences as cues for perception.

2. *Authoritarianism.* The personality pattern associated with excessive respect for and obedience to authority, admiration for power, toughness, and aggression, and an attitude of cynicism and defensive projection makes for relatively great acceptance of persuasive communication.

3. *Other-directedness.* The value system which emphasizes group adaptation and conformity leads to more persuasibility than the one which stresses personal goals and standards (inner-directedness).

4. *Social isolation.* The isolation of a child from his peers leads him to place a high value on social acceptance, accentuates an agreement-seeking process, and therefore leads to greater persuasibility.

5. *Richness of fantasy.* It is assumed that a major mechanism in attitude change is the anticipation of rewards and punishments conveyed by the communicator; thus, persons with a rich fantasy life have greater ability than others to imagine these outcomes and are therefore more receptive to persuasive communications.

6. *Sex differences.* Roles which the culture sex-types as male lead men to be more variable in their responses to pressures toward attitude change. Women, because the culture encourages them to be acquiescent, are in general more susceptible to persuasion.

The foregoing descriptions of personality factors likely to produce persuasibility should not be taken as definitive. As with all research in this area, there remains a good deal of methodological looseness and predictive uncertainty, and more questions are raised than are answered. How consistent, for example, are individual differences? Is susceptibility to mass media the same as susceptibility to interpersonal influence? While some of the research suggests that it is, the degree of relationship is not great enough for measures of persuasibility based on face-to-face situations to be of much help in predicting responsiveness to the mass media or vice versa. Obviously, further research is needed.

Another question is whether we can generalize from these findings when we consider the population samples that were used. Research has usually been carried out with college populations or middle-class urban Americans. Replication with samples representing a diversity of ethnic, class, and geographical groupings is needed to show the range of applicability of these findings. The pervasiveness of sex differences and the general dearth of explicit research on the factors underlying them is also cause for skepticism. We need to know much more about the factors responsible for these sex differences and how they relate to responsiveness to persuasive communications. The developmental factors in persuasibility also await additional research: we need to know more about how parent–child relationships and variations in patterns of child rearing give rise to variations in persuasibility.

The major question, under which all of these other questions are subsumed, is, however, "How important are personality factors as sources of individual differences in persuasibility?" The correlational data presented in *Personality and Persuasibility* suggest that they play only a minor role in determining responsiveness to pressures toward attitude change; although the correlations are positive, they are all relatively low. This does not mean, however, that there is a lack of relationship, since the low correlations may reflect low reliability or validity of the measures employed to assess both persuasibility and its personality correlates. As the editors say, however, even if there is a causal pattern, the evidence presented can be interpreted in any one of three ways: (1) the individual who feels inadequate, inferior, and a failure is motivated to conform so as to avoid social disapproval; (2) the individual who is persuasible may feel ashamed and critical of his submissiveness and so be led to feel inadequate; and (3) the individual may feel guilty about his own past actions; he may feel socially inadequate and ward off the tension associated with his inadequacy by mechanisms which give rise to a pattern of "motivated gullibility." A firmer conceptual grasp of the variables involved in the personality correlates underlying persuasibility and the testing of these formulations by controlled laboratory experimentation would certainly promote the accumulation of clearcut evidence of causal patterns.

Cognitive Needs, Cognitive Style, and Ambiguity of Communication

A somewhat different approach to the problem of individual differences stresses the role of cognitive factors in attitude change. These factors have to do with the way in which the individual goes about looking at the world around him and with his ways of dealing with the bits of information he has about himself and his environment. There is evidence that there are consistent differences between individuals in the ways in which they process the information available to them. Some people, for instance, pay little attention to the details that distinguish one item from another; others place great emphasis on details. The difference between these two kinds of people is called a difference in *cognitive style*. Many cognitive styles have been tentatively identified, each referring to a characteristic and consistent way in which some people perceive, remember, and think about aspects of themselves and the world around them. There are differences not only in style, moreover, but in *cognitive needs*. The most familiar kind of differentiation along this line involves the need to acquire knowledge: at one extreme, there are people who seem quite content to remain ignorant about anything and everything; at the other extreme, there are people who seem to have a passion to know as much as they can possibly absorb, and more.

Let us begin our consideration of cognitive factors with a much less familiar cognitive need—the need for cognitive clarity, the need to impose meaning, organization, integration, reasonableness on one's experiential world. It may be that a person develops this need because he finds that achieving clarity is instrumental in satisfying other needs and because demands are made upon him, with varying rewards and punishments for compliance and failure, to comprehend, figure out, organize, see through, and relate information. Other people may not encounter such demands, and the rewards and punishments that come to them may have little or nothing to do with whether they comprehend anything or not. Similarly, individuals may differ in the frequency with which they have found themselves in unclear, ambiguous, poorly structured situations and in the degree to which the outcomes of what they did in these situations were unpleasant, humiliating, and painful; hence, they may differ in the degree to which they learn to be frightened of ambiguity and to become anxious or "nervous" in its presence. In any case, however these differences may have arisen, people do appear to differ from one another in the strength of their needs for cognitive clarity.

What do cognitive needs have to do with attitude change? Let us return to Cohen's experiment (1957). It will be recalled that in one situation the communicator first aroused a need and then presented information helpful in satisfying it; in the other situation, the communicator used the same material but reversed the order: he presented the information first and then aroused the need. The resulting responses to a questionnaire indicated that the subjects saw these communications as differing in the degree to which they were ambiguous and lacking in cognitive clarity and reasonableness. Under these conditions, the strength of a person's cognitive need might well be a significant factor in his reaction to information given in the ambiguous, retroactive (information–need) order. His motivation to impose structure and meaning should determine the degree to which the information challenges him, even though he does not yet know what the information is relevant to.

Cohen measured the subjects' need for cognitive clarity by means of a questionnaire. He expected that while this factor would make little difference in the acceptance of the information where the communication was clear (need–information order), it would make a great deal of difference in the ambiguous order. The stronger the need, the greater should be the desire or the ability to organize the ambiguous communication, the more attention should be paid to the information, and the better should be its acquisition. Thus, when the need is later aroused, the information should be more readily available to satisfy the need and the resulting change of attitude should be greater.

When this hypothesis was tested on a college population threatened with reform of the system of grading, it was strongly confirmed. Subjects with high need for cognitive clarity changed their attitudes toward accepting the solution of grading on the curve to the same great extent whether it was offered before or after the threatening communication. When subjects with low needs for cognitive clarity received the need-arousing material first, they changed their opinions; similar students who received the information first changed less.

Cohen's experiment illustrates the usefulness of specifying a personality dimension which has direct implications for the manner in which a communication about any topic is accepted, provided that the organization of the communication can also be specified. The concept of cognitive need, however, serves only to indicate the strength of efforts toward the resolution of ambiguity, and not necessarily to identify particular modes of resolution. If, in addition to specifying the strength of efforts toward accomplishing cognitive clarity, we knew something about the person's cognitive style, we could arrive at a far more detailed picture of the relationship between personality predispositions and attitude change.

An attempt to specify cognitive style requires distinguishing between it and cognitive need. Klein (1958) and his co-workers (Gardner, Holzman, Klein, Linton, & Spence, 1959) assume that motivational states accentuate the effects of cognitive style but that different cognitive styles may in themselves have very different consequences for behavior (even among persons having the same motivation—the same strength of cognitive need). An experiment by Kelman and Cohler (1959) exemplifies this approach. As in the Cohen experiment, people with strong and weak needs for cognitive clarity were identified, but within each category of motivational strength, Kelman and Cohler specified cognitive style: persons were called either "sharpeners" (clarifiers) or "levelers" (simplifiers). "Sharpeners" are people who emphasize unique distinguishing details. If they also have a strong need for cognitive clarity, one would expect that they would become especially active in looking for cues that might eliminate ambiguity; in the process of doing so, they would, of course, open themselves up to whatever information is available. "Levelers," on the other hand, are people who operate with a limited set of cognitive categories. That is to say they characteristically ignore distinguishing details; they simplify their environment, trying to fit and even twist the content of new and distinctive experiences into familiar molds. One would expect that levelers with strong needs for cognitive clarity would react in an especially defensive way in ambiguous situations: as they normally ignore particulars, they should become especially unobservant—everything will continue to look clear and simple if they withdraw attention from whatever it is that makes the situation confusing and ignore whatever seems incongruous and whatever makes for ambiguity. Thus, the differences between levelers and sharpeners should be maximal when they have strong needs for cognitive clarity and when they find themselves in novel and unfamiliar situations.

Kelman and Cohler also anticipated that the attitudinal changes of the sharpeners would be more profound than those of the levelers. The levelers might go along with an authoritative source simply as an expedient for gaining approval, but would quickly revert to their previous attitudes; they find it easier to agree with a strong and authoritative opinion, but they will never really have comprehended it. The sharpeners, by contrast, will have opened themselves up to the substantive content of the opinion as well as to the desire of the persuader; hence, they should be more lastingly influenced, and the influence should continue to be apparent when the persuader is no longer present. These differences between levelers and sharpeners should be more or less pronounced, moreover, according to the strength of the need for cognitive clarity.

The investigators presented college students with a written persuasive communication entitled: "Our cut-rate education: removing the discount label." It was described as an article from an educational journal which appraised critically some aspects of the present education situation and offered some recommendations. It was straightforward and was assumed to offer some challenging content. The subjects, who had been measured beforehand on their need for cognitive clarity and their cognitive styles, also filled out a questionnaire on attitudes relevant to the content of the article four weeks before the communication, immediately after the communication, and again six weeks later. The questionnaire asked them about their attitudes toward the system of educational selection proposed in the communication and some of its ramifications. The person who presented the communication also administered the questionnaire immediately after the presentation. The final questionnaire six weeks later, however, was administered by a person whom the subjects had never seen before, and the questionnaire was included in a variety of other measures unrelated to the persuasive communication. In other words, the final administration was separated from the attempt at influence not only by a lapse of time but also by the absence of the influencer and by an effort to lessen the emphasis on the relevant subject matter.

As predicted, the sharpeners showed greater acceptance of

the recommendations of the communication than the levelers, and the difference was greatest for those of high need for cognitive clarity at the time of the final questionnaire. The results confirm the hypothesis that in order to understand how subjects respond to attempts at influence, one needs to know, among other things, something about their cognitive style and the strength of their motivation toward cognitive clarity and meaning.

Although Kelman identifies the difference between levelers and sharpeners in terms of "the characteristic ways in which an individual deals with situations involving ambiguity and incongruity," his experiment does not systematically vary the degree of ambiguity in the communication. He simply assumes for the purposes of his study that the communication presents a novel challenge to the subject and that any novel challenge to existing attitudes places a person in an ambiguous situation, in the sense that he has no specific previously established response to it. How well the hypothesis is supported depends on how seriously we take the assumption that the ambiguity was indeed the relevant feature of the situation. A recent experiment by Baron (1963) improves on the design. He deals with the effect of varying all three factors: the ambiguity of the communication, the need for cognitive clarity, and cognitive style.

Baron's experiment also represents another advance over earlier experiments (Cohen, 1957; Kelman & Cohler, 1959). As a result of a thorough review of the conceptual dimensions involved in the notion of need for cognitive clarity, Baron came to the conclusion that the essential feature of this need is the degree of a person's concern with the meaningfulness of all aspects of his experience; that is, some people seem to be unconcerned about the fact that they do not comprehend a great deal of what they encounter, whereas, at the other extreme, there are people who are intensely disturbed by details, no matter how trivial, that make no sense. Accepting this view of the need for cognitive clarity means that, instead of measuring it as a personality predisposition, one could manipulate it directly. Because the leveling–sharpening variable has, however, not been sufficiently studied to permit an identification of its essential dynamics, Baron had to content himself with a general measure of this variable rather than a manipulation of it.

Baron took measures of college students' cognitive styles and also of their initial attitudes toward advertising. Then, in an experimental session three weeks later, they were exposed to an extremely pro-advertising communication, purportedly written by an expert on advertising from the *Saturday Review*. For half the subjects, the material was made extremely ambiguous, with its sentences and thoughts arranged in an illogical and incoherent sequence; for the other half, the communication contained identical information but was clear, logical, and orderly. Before receiving the communication, the students were given instructions designed to produce varying needs for cognitive clarity. To produce a high need for clarity, some subjects were asked to read the communication with a great deal of attention and to give thought to its total meaning and implications. To produce low need in another group, the introduction consisted of a syntactical analysis which was less oriented toward a meaningful appraisal of the content. Measurements of the students' attitudes toward advertising were made immediately after exposure to the communication and again three weeks later.

Baron's results confirm in the main those of Kelman and Cohler. The data show that sharpeners change their attitudes more than levelers where the need is strong, but that where the need is weak, the effect is reversed, so that levelers show more attitude change than sharpeners; this effect of different needs and styles is greater where the communication is more ambiguous. Thus, as in Cohen's experiment, the effect of motivation toward clarity is greater when the communication is ambiguous, and as in Kelman and Cohler's experiment, sharpening and leveling go in one direction within one level of strength of need for clarity, in the opposite direction in the other. On the other hand, Kelman found that sharpeners showed more attitude change than levelers at the time of a delayed measurement, no matter what the strength of cognitive need, but Baron finds that his initial results remain constant even when the measurement is delayed: sharpeners change more than levelers under conditions of high need, while levelers change more than sharpeners under conditions of low need.

A great deal more experimental research is needed on these

problems before such inconsistencies as those noted can be resolved and we can fully understand the processes at work. It is clear, however, that the specification of cognitive style as well as cognitive need and the structure of the communication makes for a far more detailed picture than the one with which we began. The relationships are complex—but then the phenomena are complex. Social psychologists hope that with further research they will obtain better control of the phenomena and that they will thus be able to make finer and more accurate predictions about the conditions under which communications are accepted by people with different characteristic approaches toward the cognitive world.

Psychoanalytic Theory and Social Attitudes

In the course of our discussion of the credibility of communicators we referred to two experiments by Weiss and Fine (1955; 1956) in which they investigated certain personality factors which make for high readiness to accept a message advocating a strict, punitive attitude toward social deviants. Their findings suggest that highly aggressive persons with strong punitive tendencies toward others will be prone to adopt a strict, punitive attitude toward anyone who violates social norms. These experiments represent a view of attitude change which is both highly topic-bound and highly personality-bound; they illustrate the relationship between specified personality traits and particular persuasive communications tailored to their arousal.

More generally, however, these experiments reflect a concern with manipulation of motivational variables in studying attitude change. This research is part of an accelerating trend toward the application of advances in psychodynamic theory to the study of social attitudes (Sarnoff & Katz, 1954). This trend was clearly demonstrated in *The Authoritarian Personality* (Adorno, Frenkel-Brunswik, Levinson, & Sanford, 1950), a large-scale study of social attitudes and personality. In general, their investigation demonstrated the correspondence between certain basic psychodynamic processes characteristic of a person and his outlook on a great variety of areas, ranging from the most intimate features of family life, to sex adjustment, through relationships with other people in general, to religion, and to social and political philosophy. A great deal of research has since been done attempting to define the parameters of the relationship between personality dynamics and social phenomena. The specific application of these ideas to attitude change is, of course, the main concern here; a series of experiments by Sarnoff and his associates bear directly on their validity.

Sarnoff (1960b) discusses the relationships between motive, conflict, and ego-defense in the light of psychoanalytic theory. He interprets a motive as an internal tension-producing stimulus which is, in some form, consciously experienced by the person, who tries to act in a way that will reduce the tension. When two or more mutually inconsistent motives are activated at the same time, the person experiences conflict. He develops characteristic ways of coping with or reacting to conflict and to the constraints of his environment. Thus, when a motive impels him toward some action which may have dangerous consequences, he reacts with one or another of what are called "defense mechanisms." One such mechanism is *repression* —the individual makes himself oblivious of the motive and of anything that might bring the motive into conscious awareness. Other defense mechanisms admit the motive into consciousness, but in a distorted form. For instance, the person may make himself believe that it is not he who has this motive, but someone else (*projection*), or he may deflect the motive from its primary target (*displacement*). The defense mechanisms, however, do not reduce the tension generated by the rejected motives. They often find expression in compromise forms called *symptoms*. In this view, an attitude, which we have understood to refer to a disposition to react favorably or unfavorably to a class of objects, may be an expression of a defense mechanism, or, if it also incorporates within itself some expression of the rejected motive, it may be a type of symptom. In short, according to Sarnoff, an individual's attitude toward a class of objects is determined by the particular role those objects have come to play in facilitating responses which reduce the tension of certain motives and which resolve conflict among motives.

Several experiments illustrate the logical inference by means of which links are established between particular attitudes on the one hand and certain defense mechanisms and symptoms on the other. First, let us consider attitudes which involve projection. Psychoanalytic theory holds that by attributing his own consciously unacceptable motives to others, the individual is able to avoid perceiving them as belonging to himself. Since social prejudices involve the ascription of undesirable traits and characteristics to various groups, they would appear to be especially attractive to persons who use projection as a way of blocking their perception of their own consciously unacceptable motives. The fact that the undesirable traits ascribed to social groups which are the objects of prejudice often include sexual and aggressive motives and motives of greediness and sloppiness (all motives which are commonly rejected by people who have them) suggests that these attributions of traits are projections by people who repress their own sexual, aggressive, oral, and anal motives. In planning a series of studies on attitude change, Sarnoff and Katz (1954) based their reasoning on the notion that, insofar as consciously unacceptable motives form the basis of an individual's prejudices toward minority groups, projection may play a larger role than any of the other mechanisms of defense.

In one experiment, Katz, Sarnoff, and McClintock (1956) thought it reasonable first to use a composite measure of several defense mechanisms to classify subjects on a general dimension of resort to such mechanisms. Measurements were also made of the subjects' attitudes toward Negroes. The subjects were then exposed to two kinds of communication: some of them provided insight into the psychodynamic relationship between anti-Negro attitudes and the defense mechanisms, others provided accurate information about Negroes. After exposure, the subjects' attitudes toward Negroes were again measured and a change score was computed.

These experimenters were interested in the degree to which procedures for arousing insight can be utilized to change attitudes through mass communications. They felt that by examining the psychodynamics of prejudiced attitudes as they appear in behavior, they could gain some understanding of the relationship between defense mechanisms and attitude change. Their results showed that subjects who were prone to use defense mechanisms were not affected by the materials intended to provide insight, but that subjects who were less defensive became more favorable to Negroes after hearing the communication. Furthermore, the changes in attitude produced by the arousal of self-insight persisted longer than the changes induced by information. In other words, if the resort to the defense mechanisms is strong enough, the technique of presenting a case study revealing the dynamics of these mechanisms is relatively ineffectual; but with those whose defensiveness is lower, inducing self-insight is more effective in changing attitudes toward Negroes in a positive direction than is a rational appeal which utilizes facts and reasoned arguments.

In examining the indices which made up the ego-defensiveness score, the investigators felt that projection was the only mechanism which actually contributed to the predictive power of the over-all ego-defensiveness score. This conclusion stimulated another experiment (Katz, McClintock, & Sarnoff, 1957). In this experiment, the tendency to projection was measured separately from the other defense mechanisms; then the same experimental design used in the earlier experiment was employed. The measure of projection effectively predicted attitude change toward the Negro minority, while the measure of the other mechanisms failed to yield reliable results. The investigators conclude that the defense of projection is especially appropriate in understanding the dynamics of prejudice.

Sarnoff extended the general line of reasoning which connects conflicts and defenses to attitude change by considering a second defense mechanism, *reaction formation*. The operation of this mechanism is inferred when a person acts as though he wants the exact opposite of what is taken to be an unacceptable motive, but is betrayed by his overreaction (he "doth protest too much, methinks").

Sarnoff (1960a) took cynicism as especially relevant to the defense of reaction formation against a consciously unacceptable motive of affection for others. (To love one's neighbor may have the dangerous consequence of opening oneself to exploitation.) A person who uses reaction formation as a defense against his unconscious feelings of affection ought to behave coolly, even perhaps with hostility, toward others. By accepting skeptical and uncomplimentary views of human nature—by the acceptance of a cynical attitude—he can respond more readily toward others with coolness and remain unaware that actually he has affectionate feelings for them. Sarnoff reasoned that, since an intense arousal of affection evokes more anxiety in individuals with a strong reaction formation against affection than among those whose reaction formation is weak, the former should change their attitudes more, to become more cynical as the intensity of affection-arousing stimuli increases.

To test this hypothesis he measured subjects' tendencies toward reaction formation against affectionate feelings. At the same time, he administered an attitude scale measuring cynicism. The communications which served to arouse the subjects' affectionate feelings were two versions of a dramatic presentation, "live" to half of the subjects and tape-recorded to the other half, of William Saroyan's play *Hello Out There*. The scene adapted for the experiment was a tender, affectionate, emotional one. In the live presentation, the affection was played up; in the taped version, it was played down. Following the performance, the measure of cynicism was given again to the subjects and a measure of attitude change was derived from the differences in their responses from before to after the presentation.

The results showed that both groups of subjects tended to become less cynical after the play, but the degree to which the presentation affected them was different for the two groups: the change in the subjects high in reaction formation was less than in the others. This differential effect was greater under the conditions of high arousal (live play) than under the conditions of low arousal (tape recording). While the findings are consistent with the postulated relationship between reaction formation and change on the attitude dimension of cynicism, they might be more parsimoniously interpreted by assuming that cynicism is a directly learned pattern rather than a reaction formation: the stronger the habit, the more resistant it is to change.

A final illustration of Sarnoff's approach to personality and attitude change concerns the investigation of attitudes which facilitate overt symptomatic responses to the tensions of consciously unacceptable motives. In this experiment (Sarnoff & Corwin, 1959) the investigators deal directly with psychosexual conflicts rather than with defense mechanisms associated with them. Specifically, the aim of this experiment was to test an hypothesis concerning the relationship between unconscious fear of castration and attitudes toward death (fear of death). The authors expected that persons who have a high degree of castration anxiety would show a greater change in their attitudes in the direction of fearing death after arousal of their sexual feelings than persons who have a low degree of castration anxiety. According to psychoanalytic theory, a sexually arousing stimulus which has become associated with punishment during the critical years of childhood may lead to castration anxiety when the individual is confronted with the stimulus in later life. Castration anxiety can be manifested in fears of bodily injury and, in its extreme form, in fears of death. Thus, when aroused by sexual feelings, castration anxiety may be reflected on the attitudinal level as increasing fear of death.

This hypothesis was tested by a before-and-after experimental design which provided for the arousal of two levels of sexual feeling among subjects of high and low castration anxiety, as measured before the experiment. Attitude measures were taken on a "fear of death" scale administered before and after the sexual arousal. The manipulation of arousal was accomplished by showing pictures of nude women (for the condition of high arousal) and of fully clothed women (for the condition of low arousal) under the guise of a study in esthetics. The data clearly confirm the hypothesis: the attitude-change scores from before to after sexual arousal show that the subjects with high castration anxiety experienced a greater increase in their fear of death than did the subjects with low castration anxiety. As expected, this difference was greater under conditions of high arousal than of low.

All four experiments in this series were carried out within the framework of an approach to attitude change which assumes a functional connection between certain constellations of psychosexual conflict and ego-defense and certain specific social attitudes. The results are sufficiently promising to warrant further exploration of this domain of inquiry.

Taking into account the entire body of results regarding the relationship between personality and persuasibility, we can see how a complete matrix might be developed to show how certain personality factors interact with certain processes of persuasion to produce one or another effect. That is to say, some personality variables such as low self-esteem or high anxiety might affect learning of the persuasive communication and thus affect attitude change; others, like a certain ego-defense or cognitive style, might affect retention; and still others might affect acceptance. Thus, the relationship between the person and the communication in producing attitude change is certainly no simple matter, once we consider the manifold possibilities involved in such an approach. Nevertheless, the totality of such relationships in all their complexity is central to our understanding of attitude change.

Up to this point, we have dealt mainly with situations in which an external communicator attempted to influence a person taken as an isolated unit. The foregoing analysis of the determinants and effects of this situation can be called, in general, a molar one, that is to say, it was concerned with what effect messages had depending on the organization of the message, the kind of communicator, and some qualities of the recipient. Except, perhaps, in the discussion of some of the material on personality, we have not looked very closely at what happened inside the person's psychic structure as the messages came in, nor have we examined the psychological processes by which the person made an adjustment or a compromise between his initial position or the information he possessed and the new position or new information presented by the communicator. The following chapter takes a closer, more molecular approach to the processes which facilitate the adjustments or compromises (attitude changes) that people make when they are confronted with information discrepant from an attitude or position they hold.

5

COGNITIVE MODELS
OF ATTITUDE CHANGE

THE NEXT STEP in analyzing attitude change is to look more closely at psychological structure—the organized set of cognitions a person has about himself and the world around him. Let us try to follow the course of a persuasive communication as it enters that cognitive structure and examine the ways in which it affects it and thereby produces attitudinal change.

The earlier discussion has omitted the notion of inconsistency between an initial attitudinal structure and new information in the interests of the examination of the more formal aspects of communication, communicator, and communicatee. Now, however, it is time to introduce the principle of cognitive consistency, a principle based on the notion that psychological structure is composed of an integrated, organized set of cognitions regarding some object or event. The introduction of new information aimed at changing attitudes disrupts that organization and produces disequilibrium. The problem, then, is to understand just how an adjustment is made between the ongoing structure and the new information so that equilibrium is again achieved. A number of very interesting consequences for theory and research follow from such an orientation.

Cognition denotes the image or map of the world held by the

individual person. His responses to persons, things, and events are shaped in part by the way they look to him. These cognitions are selectively organized and integrated into a system which provides meaning and stability for the individual person as he goes about his business in the everyday world. Thus, human cognitive reactions like perceiving, thinking, imagining, and reasoning all represent efforts after meaning. In terms of the person's cognitive system, therefore, there is a continual striving for consistency, a push toward congruous, harmonious, fitting relationships between the cognitive elements or between the thoughts, beliefs, values, and actions that make up a structure of cognitions about some object or set of events. Thus, when inconsistency occurs, some psychological tension is presumably set up in the individual, thereby motivating his behavior in the direction of reducing this inconsistency and reestablishing harmony. In effect, the cognitive process constantly strives toward cognitive balance.

Although it is generally true that a person tends to make various aspects of his cognitive functioning consistent with one another, it cannot be said that all systems achieve perfect consistency. The human mind is so complex and has available to it so many compartmentalizations, rationalizations, and other defense mechanisms that the principle of consistency is not a uniformly accurate predictor of attitude change. Even if there are some limits to this principle, however, it is a powerful predictive tool.

Let us consider an example of just how this motivation for consistency operates in someone going about his daily affairs. Suppose you are a businessman who prides himself on his climb up the ladder of success and believes strongly in all the virtues associated with a democratic free-enterprise society. You are against powerful labor organizations, you despise socialism, and your ego-ideals are other businessmen who have reached an even more impressive point in life. You would certainly expect to like another person who shares your likes and dislikes, and to believe that the person you like does in fact share your likes and dislikes. Thus your attitudes do, indeed, have some consistency: you like him and he shares your likes and dislikes; your likes and dislikes are consistent with one another and his likes and dislikes are consistent with one another. Furthermore, to have a highly consistent set of cognitions, you should believe that a third person whom you dislike would like the things you despise. Therefore it should not surprise you that a neighbor with whom you have had a great deal of trouble over the loan of a lawn mower believes in numerous "socialistic practices" like Medicare and federal control of railroads. To be still more consistent, you should also feel that the man you admire and with whom you are friendly also dislikes this third person. Furthermore, you should expect both of you to like a fourth person whom you have never met, should you hear from a mutual friend that this new person also dislikes the trend toward "government control" and is himself a highly successful businessman. You would be certain that you were both going to like him if you also learned that he and the man with whom you had the argument about the lawn mower disliked each other intensely.

The ramifications of perfect consistency would spin out endlessly, but these illustrations are enough. The next question is "What happens when new information enters the system?" If it adds another link of cognitions in the same direction, there is no difficulty. Suppose, however, our businessman learns that his respected friend thinks the Russian system of farm collectivization is efficient and practical, raises the standard of living, and should be considered for adoption here. What if he hears that the president of a powerful union is a major force in holding the line against "creeping socialism"? What if, during his backyard interchanges with his neighbor, he finds out that the neighbor has been invited to the house of his respected friend, or that the neighbor he has maligned as "soft on socialism" never really held those views at all? What if one day when he returns from the office early, he discovers the despised neighbor's wife having a late afternoon cocktail with his wife? All of these new bits of information represent cognitions inconsistent with those he already holds, and they create a good deal of disequilibrium in him. "How is it possible," he says, "for X, whom I like and admire, to be favorable toward Russia, which I despise?" "How can my neighbor whom I think a jackass," he wonders, "be in favor of the same set of government restrictions that I am and be respected by the man I most respect?" This sort of disequilibrium initiates changes in the businessman's cognitive structure, and these changes are directed toward the restoration of equilibrium.

The changes are numerous, varied, of different degrees of effectiveness, and often obscure. All of the theoretical models we shall discuss deal with changes toward the restoration of consistency, though they often focus on different modes and specify different theoretical determinants of resolution. In the present context, their specification of the conditions under which the modes and degrees of resolution of cognitive inconsistency occur can contribute toward an understanding of the determinants of attitude change. The models all have as their starting point the principle of consistency–inconsistency, though the investigators use different terms to designate them. The following discussion will treat first the congruity–incongruity model, then the balance–imbalance model, and finally the consonance–dissonance model. Although they have a good deal in common, there are critical differences among them which have different consequences for theory and research. The interested reader may follow up the present brief review of these models in the original sources, or in the discussions by Katz (1960) and Brown (1962).

The Principle of Congruity

Associated with the congruity model are the names of Charles Osgood and his associates, George Suci and Percy Tannenbaum. In their scheme, a given object is first evaluated on a scale which runs from *good* to *bad*. Since a person has an infinitude of attitudes toward a variety of objects, some of his evaluations will be consistent with one another, others inconsistent. Thus, admiration of President Kennedy could have been consistent with a strong belief in the value of physical fitness; the assertion that President Kennedy favored the promotion of physical fitness is then a congruent cognition. It is possible to hold varying attitudes toward diverse concepts without incongruity so long as these objects are not brought into relation with one another. For example, one could have felt favorably toward President Kennedy and also have disliked the idea of a farm program which decreased subsidies to farmers. But once an associative bond linked President Kennedy and the farm program so that one had the cognition that President Kennedy *was in favor of* a revised farm program, incongruity would motivate the individual to make his cognitions internally consistent. In sum, for Kennedy to come out in favor of a program for physical fitness was congruent with this person's attitudes toward both; for Kennedy to have come out with a new farm program would have been incongruent. Osgood's congruity model describes this process as a basic way in which human thinking operates: that sources we like should always denounce ideas we are against and support ideas we are for.

If the existence of incongruity results in pressure to reduce it, the process is one of attitude change. When two attitudinal objects which have evaluative (good–bad) signs associated with them are brought into an incongruent relationship, the pressure to regain congruence leads to a change in the evaluation of one or the other or both of them. For example, if Kennedy, who was admired, had made a favorable assertion about increasing income taxes, which we abhor, the most general pressure on us would have been to evaluate Kennedy less favorably and to view the prospect of a rise in income taxes more favorably. In effect, if both concept and source move toward a more neutral point, the result is less incongruity in the over-all cognition.

From Osgood's model, however, one can be more specific about the direction of attitude change and about which object will change most. The major factor is the degree to which the object is polarized. If Kennedy was seen as at the extreme "good" end of the good–bad scale and tax rises were seen as at only a moderately bad position on the scale, taxes would move toward Kennedy and the person would end up being somewhat more favorable toward the prospect of increased income taxes. Conversely, if the person was evaluatively rather neutral toward tax rises but could not bear Kennedy, the relatively neutral prospect of increased taxes would become less favorable. Finally, if we had no feelings for Kennedy one way or another and we heard that he supported physical fitness, which we favor, we would change our attitudes so that we liked him more, while if we learned that he favored a detestable farm program, we would grow to dislike him.

In an experiment by Tannenbaum (1953), the aim was to show that persuasive communications would be effective in changing evaluations (producing attitude change) depending upon the subject's initial attitudes toward the source of the communications and toward the object or issue. Three source-object pairs were selected: labor leaders with legalized gambling, the Chicago *Tribune* with abstract art, and Senator Robert Taft with accelerated college programs. Subjects who were college students first evaluated the six objects on attitude scales which ran from "good" to "bad." A number of weeks later, they were exposed to communications ("highly realistic newspaper stories") which linked members of the pairs. The communications included positive or negative assertions about the source-concept pairs. For example, some subjects were told that the Chicago *Tribune* was a great supporter of modern art, others were told that the *Tribune* decried the contemporary trends in art; some subjects were told that Taft favored an accelerated college program, others that he stood firmly against it, and so forth. It was expected that, depending upon the initial attitudes toward one or the other member of a pair and depending upon the relative extremity or polarization, attitudes toward one or the other of the pair would change in one direction or the other in response to the assertion which linked them (the persuasive communication).

The results showed that attitudes toward objects change in a positive direction when communications link them with highly valued sources and change in a negative direction when they are linked with disliked sources. If the *Tribune* is admired, then attitudes toward abstract art change in a positive direction if the *Tribune* is seen to favor abstract art. On the other hand, if Taft is despised, his advocacy of an accelerated college program will lead to a change in attitude so that the college program is seen as less beneficial than it had been earlier. Conversely, if abstract art is disliked by the subject and the college program is seen as highly desirable, there will be some change in the direction of negative attitudes toward the *Tribune* and positive attitudes toward Taft.

On the other hand, when the source is disliked, the change of attitude toward an issue is in the positive direction when the bond is dissociative—when it is clear that the source has repudiated the object. Similarly, when a source that is admired repudiates an object, attitudes toward that object change in a negative direction, so that it becomes more disliked. In addition, attitude change is inversely proportional to the extremity or polarization of the attitude on the good–bad scale. Thus, if the person's attitude toward abstract art is extremely positive and he is only moderately favorable toward the *Tribune,* his attitudes toward the *Tribune* will change more (in the negative direction) than his attitudes toward abstract art if the *Tribune* condemns abstract art.

The congruity model approaches the study of the effects of persuasive communications by focusing on the links between sources toward which one has an attitude and objects toward which one has an attitude. When assertions made by persuasive communications produce incongruous relationships between sources and objects, attitudes change; and they change in the direction of increased congruity depending upon the sign and extremity of the initial attitudes toward the two members of the linked pair.

Osgood (1960) gives a compelling descriptive account of the widespread significance of the phenomena of cognitive congruity-incongruity. If a Russian diplomat, for example, makes a sweeping proposal for world disarmament, it is immediately seen as a carefully planned move in the Cold War; it is cognitively inconsistent for us to think of people we dislike and mistrust as making honest, sincere conciliatory moves. A man who we are told is intelligent, warm, and considerate is inferred to be also sensitive, admirable, and alert, rather than narrow, self-seeking, and withdrawn. If an FBI agent speaks before a local citizens' group in a university town and asserts that the university has never invited an anti-Communist to lecture, many people in the audience will conclude, even though no direct allegation has been made, that pro-Communists have been invited to speak or that the university has some influential Communists on its staff. A man who is favorably disposed toward Nixon both as a person and as a potential President will develop different attitudes about South American countries toward which he has been hitherto neutral depending upon how Nixon is received there. If in one country students boo Nixon and pelt him with fruit, the person will develop negative attitudes toward that country, whereas if Nixon is well received in another country, the person will find himself considerably more favorable toward it. Furthermore, there will be a tendency to discount subsequent information that the latter country suffers under a harsh dictatorship, whereas the former has a democratic form of government similar to our own. As all these examples show, we strive to maintain internal consistency among our attitudes, and what attitude changes we experience as well as the facts we can assimilate operate in the direction of establishing consistency.

The Balance Model

Another general model which represents attitude change in terms of the push to resolve inconsistency between cognitions is the one that centers around the notion of balance (Heider, 1958). Its basic postulate is that if people seek balance or congruence between their beliefs and their feelings about objects, then their attitudes can be changed by modifying either the beliefs or the feelings. A study by Rosenberg (1956) showed general congruity to exist between feelings and beliefs (between affect and cognition) and an experiment by Carlson (1956) showed that when incongruity is aroused between feeling and belief, the result can be the feeling's changing so as to become consistent with the altered belief. Thus, the affective component of an attitude (the aspect of evaluation) can change in the direction of consistency with changed beliefs or cognitions regarding that object. This effect is not difficult to understand: if we have certain beliefs about an object or issue and learn that they may cause benefit or harm, our feelings about it will change accordingly. The other side of the coin, however, is less obvious: How do beliefs come to change it feelings are changed? This more obscure aspect of the push to-ward cognitive consistency was explored experimentally by Rosenberg (1960).

Rosenberg assumed that the disruption of structural consist-ency (consistency between affective and belief components of an attitude) is a basic condition for the occurrence of atti-tude change. Disruption will culminate in a general reorganiza-tion of attitude which operates to reduce the affective–cognitive inconsistency. Through the use of hypnosis, Rosenberg felt he could manipulate a subject's affective feelings without in-terference from attendant cognitions. If beliefs then changed, he could assume that it was pure affect which caused the change and that it was not the result of a direct attack on the belief itself. In this fashion he hoped to test his theoretical model, which postulates that beliefs about an object will change when feelings about that object change, and that it is the stress toward cognitive consistency which produces the change of attitude.

In one of his experiments, Rosenberg gave subjects a ques-tionnaire which measured their affective responses to social issues; for example, how much they liked or disliked the idea of Negroes moving into white neighborhoods. The subjects were then measured for their cognitive structure (the degree to which the issue served to meet or frustrate their desires and values). For example, a person might be much concerned with the worth of his property (value) and think that desegregation of housing would lower the worth of his property (block the attainment of his value). After this measurement, experimental subjects were then hypnotized and commanded to *feel* dif-ferently about the object. Taking the same example, they were told, "When you awake, you will be very much in favor of the idea of Negroes moving into white neighborhoods; the mere thought will make you happy." Subjects were told that they would have no memory of the suggestion's having been made until a signal was given, and upon awakening from hypnosis they were once again given the measure of cognitive structure. The results showed that the hypnotized subjects did indeed change their beliefs to be consistent with their hypnotically induced feelings: they now felt that the prospect of Negroes moving into white neighborhoods was less likely to lower property values. This result was in contrast to the results found using control subjects who merely rested in the same physical setting as the experimental subjects or who were asked to role-play a change in their attitudes by "behaving like a person who feels one thing and believes another." Thus, when the affective component of an individual's attitude is altered, there occurs a corresponding and consistent reorganization of beliefs about the objects of that affect.

One of the difficulties with hypnosis is that few people are acceptable subjects. It is relatively easy, however, for most people to play a role which draws on their past experiences, and it is this role-playing technique which was used by Rosenberg and Abelson (1960) in another, more elaborate experimental test of the balance model. The specific application of their model to attitude change rests on the notion that if a cognitive structure is unbalanced, and the person becomes aware of the inconsistency, he may attempt to resolve the imbalance by changing either the relations between the elements or the signs associated with the elements or both. These changes represent what we have been referring to as attitudinal changes. In their test of the balance model, the investigators focused on the degree to which the person who has an unbalanced set of cognitions "thinks" his way through to cognitive balance—changes his attitudes—when he is presented new information.

The investigators "implanted" cognitive dilemmas in their undergraduate subjects by role-playing. Three groups of subjects were presented a pamphlet which invited them to take the role of a department-store owner who placed positive value on keeping sales high. Subjects in one of the groups were told that they felt positively toward both modern art and the manager of the rug department, a certain Fenwick. For the second group, modern art was positive and Fenwick negative, and for the third group, both Fenwick and modern art were given negative signs. All subjects were then given "facts" (the persuasive communication) to support the following beliefs: displays of modern art in department stores reduce the volume of sales,

Fenwick plans to display modern art in the rug department, Fenwick's management has in the past increased sales of rugs. Thus, all three groups had assigned to them identical cognitive relationships so far as asserted relations were concerned, but with varied evaluations of the things related. Three groups with different cognitive structures were thereby set up, each unbalanced in a different way. In the first, high volume of sales is desirable, Fenwick is a fine fellow, he has a past record of increasing sales, modern art is fine, Fenwick is going to show modern art. But—modern art will decrease sales. In the second structure, with modern art positively evaluated, the belief that Fenwick is going to display modern art is unbalanced. In the third structure, high volume of sales is desirable, Fenwick is undesirable, modern art is undesirable, its display decreases sales, Fenwick is going to display it. But—he has a past record of increasing sales.

The subjects were then presented three countercommunications which supposedly issued from three officers of the store. Each of these presented information which, if accepted, would lead to the least effortful solution for one of the three unbalanced structures—a solution involving only one change in relation. The results show that a communication stating that displays of modern art increase sales was accepted by subjects in group one. By accepting it, the subjects ended up with a consistent and pleasant set of beliefs: that fine fellow Fenwick is really doing the right thing after all and will increase sales. The results for the other groups, however, showed that not only do subjects look for a solution that requires the least effort in order to attain balance and consistency, but they also seek the solution that maximizes gain and minimizes potential loss: the one that is associated with the most pleasantness.

The balance model expounded by Rosenberg and Abelson assumes, then, that persuasive communications will be accepted by the person (or at least will be seen by him as pleasant and persuasive even if his attitudes do not actually change) to the degree that they help resolve cognitive imbalances. The specific conditions under which the principles of least effort and hedonic gain act in concert or in opposition to determine acceptance await the results of further experimentation. Rosenberg and

Abelson's research represents an attempt to provide experimental tests of the balance hypothesis, to extend it to attitude change, and to consider its applicability to the complex cognitive processes that actually go on in people's minds.

The Theory of Cognitive Dissonance

The third cognitive model for dealing with the effects of persuasive communication is the consonance–dissonance model. Cognitive dissonance, according to Festinger (1957), is a psychological tension having motivational characteristics. The theory of cognitive dissonance concerns itself with the conditions that arouse dissonance in an individual and with the ways in which dissonance can be reduced.

The relation that exists between two elements is said to be consonant if one implies the other in some psychological sense. Psychological implication may arise from cultural mores, pressure to be logical, behavioral commitment, past experience, and so on. What is meant by implication is that having a given cognition, A, leads to having another given cognition, B. The detection of psychological implication is frequently possible by measurement of what else a person expects when he holds a given cognition.

A dissonant relationship exists between two cognitive elements when a person possesses one which follows from the obverse of another that he possesses—one that is *not* implied by the other. Thus, if A implies B, then holding A and the obverse of B is dissonant. A person experiences dissonance, a motivational tension, when he has cognitions among which there are one or more dissonant relationships. Cognitive elements that are neither dissonant nor consonant with each other are said to be irrelevant.

The amount of dissonance associated with a given cognition is a function of the importance of that cognition and of the one with which it is dissonant. The magnitude of dissonance is also a function of the ratio of dissonant to consonant cognitions, where each cognitive element is weighted for its importance to the person. As the number or importance, or both, of dissonant cognitions increases relative to the number or importance, or both, of consonant cognitions, the magnitude of dissonance increases.

In general, a person may reduce dissonance by decreasing the number or importance, or both, of dissonant elements compared to consonant elements, or he may reduce the importance of all relevant elements together. It should be noted that propositions about the magnitude of dissonance can be tested without there being any actual reduction of dissonance, since a state of dissonance leads to attempts at the reduction of dissonance rather than necessarily to successful reduction.

How dissonance is reduced (or attempts at reduction are made) depends on the resistance to change of relevant cognitive elements. Those cognitions with relatively low resistance tend to change first. The resistance to change of a cognitive element comes from the extent to which a change would produce new dissonance and from some joint function of the anchorage of the cognition in reality (what it represents) and the difficulty of changing the reality. Where the reality represented is ambiguous (a diffuse emotional reaction to oneself, a physical stimulus in the presence of considerable noise, or the prediction of an uncertain future event), the cognitive element can be changed quite readily without any change in the reality. On the other hand, if the reality is quite clear, then the resistance to change of the corresponding cognitive element will generally be proportional to the difficulty of changing the reality. How difficult it is to change a given aspect of reality varies all the way from extremely easy to essentially impossible. For example, it is frequently quite easy for a person to change his behavior, as when he finds he has entered the wrong word in a crossword puzzle. Or, to take the opposite extreme, he may find it impossible to change the fact that he has lost a gift having considerable sentimental value. It is, of course, undeniable that where reality is difficult or even impossible to change, the corresponding cognitive element can still be changed by making it inconsistent with reality, but by and large there appears to be an overwhelming pressure for people to keep their cognitions consistent with reality.

The specific application of this model to attitudinal change necessitates a consideration of the pressure on a person to reduce the dissonance occasioned by his having certain cognitions about an object while other, dissonant ones are introduced by a new communication or the person's own behavior, or both. The degree to which the dissonant cognitions outweigh the consonant ones is the degree to which dissonance and consequent attempts at the reduction of dissonance will occur. To the extent that dissonance can be reduced by changing one or another cognition (attitude), persuasive communications advocating changes in those cognitions will be accepted. When one engages in behavior vis-à-vis a communicator or a persuasive communication that is counter to one's initial attitude, the dissonance between the behavior and the initial attitude can be resolved in favor of changing the attitude in the direction of the communication, since the completed behavior is more resistant to change. Where the communicator or the behavior can be repudiated, attitude change in the direction of the persuasive communication may not take place.

An example will illustrate how the theory works. Suppose that we wish to induce a child to eat a vegetable he dislikes. Since a person does not ordinarily eat a vegetable he dislikes, one way to accomplish this end would be to offer the child a reward for eating a serving of the vegetable. It is clear, of course, that the reward must be sufficiently attractive to overcome the child's reluctance to eat. Assuming that it is, and that the child has been induced to eat, what can we say about the child's behavior in terms of the theory of dissonance?

Knowledge that one has eaten a vegetable clearly follows from the obverse of knowledge that one dislikes the vegetable, and these two elements are therefore dissonant with each other. On the other hand, knowledge that one has received a reward for having eaten the vegetable is clearly consonant with the knowledge that one has eaten the vegetable. Since the child's dislike of the vegetable is dissonant with his behavior of eating it, the child will experience dissonance. The amount of the dissonance will be a direct function of the importance of the dissonant cognitive element (the amount of dislike for the vegetable) compared to the importance of the consonant cognitive element (the amount of reward obtained for having eaten the vegetable).

Again, clear implications follow from this formulation, two in particular: the greater the initial dislike for the vegetable, the greater the magnitude of dissonance; the greater the reward for having eaten it, the smaller the magnitude of dissonance.

The child could conceivably reduce the dissonance he experiences in a number of ways. The way which most concerns us here is that of attitude change. Thus the child might try to reduce dissonance by changing his attitude—by increasing his liking for the vegetable, and thereby making the formerly dissonant element consonant. He might also try to magnify the value of the reward, thereby making the dissonant element relatively unimportant. Finally, he might try to reduce the relative importance of his dislike for the vegetable.

In an experiment which illustrates the application of dissonance theory to the study of attitude change (Cohen, 1959b), the investigator put subjects to work trying to understand a communication which they knew supported a position counter to their own. Since working on the discrepant communication would follow from the obverse of the attitude they initially held, we would expect dissonance to be produced. Furthermore, the harder they worked on the communication, the greater the dissonance, since there are fewer cognitions which support hard work on a position one is against than support doing little work. In addition, the more negative one is, the more dissonance should one experience, since if one is strongly opposed to a position, there may be still less reason for working hard to understand it than if one is only mildly opposed. Thus, Cohen predicted that greater dissonance and consequently greater acceptance of the communication so as to reduce that dissonance would occur where the subjects were strongly opposed and where they had worked hard to understand the communication. By becoming more favorable toward the position, one makes consonant one's having worked hard over it when one is strongly opposed to it. The results showed that those subjects whose initial position was strongly opposed and who expended relatively great effort in trying to understand the communication opposing their private attitude apparently experienced more dissonance, as indicated by their greater attitude change toward accepting the initially unacceptable position.

Another experiment (Zimbardo, 1963) provides additional support for the notion that working hard over a contrary position produces dissonance and that this dissonance can be reduced by coming to accept the position. Zimbardo chose subjects who were all strongly in favor of their university's adopting a numerical system of grading and told them that they would have to read a report which was in fact a series of arguments against the numerical system of grading which they favored. To create variations in dissonance, half of the subjects read the report under conditions of high effort, while half read it under conditions of low effort. Effort was manipulated by having the subjects read the report aloud under varying conditions of delayed auditory feedback: to create a situation requiring high effort, subjects experienced a delay interval of 0.3 second; for low effort, a delay interval of 0.01 second. The 0.3-second delay, compared with the 0.01-second delay, creates more disruption of the subject's speech, makes comprehension more difficult, and hence increases the effort necessary to perform adequately. Results indicated that the subjects who had to exert high effort became significantly more opposed to numerical grading (to their original stand) than the subjects who exerted less effort.

A related experiment illustrates the effect of choosing to expose oneself to a communication one knows is counter to one's attitudes (Cohen, Terry, & Jones, 1959). Choosing to expose oneself to opposed opinions surely does not follow from a negative attitude toward the issue; since, however, it does follow from the obverse of such an initial attitude, it should produce dissonance. Since the more negative one is toward an issue, the less it follows that one should choose to expose oneself, the result should be greater dissonance and consequently greater attitude change the more strongly opposed the initial attitude. The data showed that among persons who were extreme in their opposition to the position of the communication, those who chose to expose themselves to the discrepant communication showed greater change toward the position of the communication than did those who had little choice. Thus the data support the notion that dissonance is a direct function of choice in adopting a contrary attitude position.

A variation of the basic derivation that inconsistent information creates dissonance is the hypothesis that the magnitude of dissonance is a direct function of the *degree* of inconsistency. Evidence about inconsistency and the importance of issues as determinants of the magnitude of dissonance comes from a study of Zimbardo (1960). Pairs of friends were led to believe that they disagreed either a little or a lot in their judgments of a case study of juvenile delinquency. The importance of the rating of the case was varied by telling some pairs that their judgments represented basic values, personality traits, and outlook on important life problems and by telling other pairs that their judgments did not mean much.

Dissonance aroused by learning that the judgment made by one's friend disagrees with one's own judgment can easily be reduced or eliminated by changing one's own judgment. Hence, if dissonance increases as discrepancy and importance increase, then change in judgment toward the friend's more acceptable position should also increase. It was found that change toward the friend's position is directly proportional to the amount of discrepancy and to the importance of the issue. These results therefore lend support to the notion that active exposure to information discrepant with one's own view creates dissonance.

Another bit of evidence on the effects of active exposure to discrepant information is available from a study by Brehm (1960). He showed that junior high school students, committed to eating either a little or a lot of a disliked vegetable, tended, in proportion to the amount of eating, to accept a communication claiming that the vegetable was high in vitamin content and to reject a communication claiming that the vegetable was low in vitamin content. Thus, where the communication tended to decrease dissonance, opinion changed, and, where the communication tended to increase dissonance, opinion tended not to change.

Dissonance theory, in addition to its relevance for attitude change under conditions of active exposure, also bears on the problem of the conditions under which a person will choose to attend to attitude-discrepant information. Another way of reducing the dissonance occurring after a decision or behavioral act is to expose oneself to further information which is likely to justify the decision taken; in other words, to reduce the dissonance. Although the results are somewhat equivocal, studies by Adams (1961), Ehrlich, Guttman, Schönbach, and Mills (1957), Mills, Aronson, and Robinson (1959), and Rosen (1961) all provide evidence relevant to the notion that persons actively seek additional information (acquire new cognitions) in order to reduce dissonance. This phenomenon of differential exposure is important for understanding the process of attitude change because through selective exposure a person can maintain his current attitudes and protect his beliefs, values, and self-image. We should generally expect attitude change to be reduced to the degree that attention to persuasive communications is lessened through differential exposure. Dissonance theory helps to pinpoint some of the conditions under which differential exposure to attitude-discrepant persuasive communications occurs.

These studies all illustrate the applicability of the dissonance formulation of attitude change. Unlike the other formulations of inconsistency we have discussed, the theory of dissonance contains no assignment of positive, negative, or neutral signs to cognitive elements in and of themselves. Rather, it stresses the notion of psychological implication and assumes that dissonance results from the fact that one element follows from the obverse of another. More importantly, the dissonance formulation is unique in that it has something special to say about individual *behavior,* and it is this behavioral commitment that allows us to fix unequivocally the existence of dissonance. Thus, while the balance and incongruity models are mainly concerned with inconsistent cognitions related to objects or events in the environment, the dissonance model focuses on the individual's own behavior as that behavior serves to create dissonance between groups of his cognitions.

All three theories based on inconsistency have implications for understanding a person's response to persuasive communications in that they focus on the ways in which persuasive communications disrupt cognitive structure and on the means which they provide for resolving inconsistency. Thus, attitude change may be analyzed in terms of a strain toward consistency and the enhanced acceptance of any communication which facilitates this attempt. Where persons are confronted with incoming environmental information, as with most propaganda or social influence, all three theories present complementary, if competing, models for understanding when attitudes will change and when they will not. Because of its unique emphasis on the individual's behavior in creating dissonance for himself as he engages in behavior discrepant from his cognitions, however, the dissonance model is uniquely equipped to explain the effects of situations where the person is induced to do or say something he does not want to do or say. The next chapter will describe situations of enforced compliant behavior, and, through the dissonance formulation, will attempt to analyze the conditions under which forced compliance will be more or less effective in producing attitude change. The dissonance model, which stresses the effects of behavior on attitudes, is especially appropriate for studying the situation in which compliance is enforced.

6

THE EFFECTS OF
ENFORCED DISCREPANT
BEHAVIOR

AN AMERICAN prisoner of war in Korea who longs for a smoke
agrees to read a prepared indictment of American foreign policy
before a group of fellow prisoners, on the promise of a cigarette.
Another prisoner, an Air Force major who has had no news
from home and who has been promised his letters, makes a
statement before cameras that there were strange-looking
bombs, perhaps germ bombs, strapped on the wings of his plane
when he took off on a bombing mission. A reform Democrat in
New York who despises bossism endorses the platform of a
Tammany leader who seeks re-election, in the hope that the
party's support will be thrown to him for his own campaign in
the next election. A Southern girl in a liberal New England
girls' college finds herself publicly agreeing with her roommates'
views on school and residential racial integration. An American
dissident on a trip to Europe vociferously defends American
values and the American way of life before a group of scornful
left-wing café intellectuals.

What do all these people have in common? It is obvious that
all of them, for one reason or inducement or another, are saying
or doing something contrary to their private attitudes. In formal

terms, their cognitions concerning the initial attitude they held and their subsequent behavior are in a dissonant relationship. As indicated in the preceding chapter, when a person possesses a cognition about his behavior that follows from the obverse of the belief he holds, dissonance results. As dissonance is psychologically uncomfortable, we should expect these people to experience some psychological tension. This uncomfortable psychological tension will motivate them to reduce the tension—to reduce that dissonance so as to achieve consonance. We should therefore expect all of the people mentioned to engage in some cognitive modification aimed at reducing the dissonance between their attitudes and their behavior. It is this push to reduce dissonance that results in attitude change in situations of enforced discrepant behavior.

Dissonance theory is especially appropriate for the study of the sorts of situation described above, where persons are "forced" to comply with a request that they behave in a way that does not follow from their cognitions. Because of its emphasis on postdecision behavior, this model can focus on the *consequences* of the decision to comply with the discrepant request insofar as attitudes are affected. Through its *specification of the ratio of dissonant to consonant cognitions,* it can identify the magnitude of the dissonance resulting from engaging in discrepant behavior; in other words, it will permit an assessment of the forces leading toward and away from the discrepant behavior. Given the magnitude of dissonance, the strength of efforts to reduce it may be identified; thus, if attitude change is the preferred mode of reducing dissonance, the degree of change may safely be predicted. And finally, the fact that *behavioral commitment* is a central aspect of the analysis based on the dissonance formulation allows us to be sure that we can focus on attitudinal change; commitment is to the relatively irrevocable discrepant behavior, so that when dissonance is reduced it can only be reduced through the change of attitudes so that they become consonant with the discrepant behavior.

If a person is led to express outwardly an attitude which is discrepant from his actual private attitude, a state of dissonance results. Since the behavior is fixed, dissonance in such a setting can be reduced by changing one's attitude so that it becomes consistent with the behavior one has engaged in publicly. There is no dissonance remaining because private attitude and public expression are now consistent with each other.

Two of the earliest experimental studies illustrating this proposition, though not intended specifically to test it, were carried out by Janis and King (1954; 1956). They asked college students either to present, as sincerely as possible, a speech from a prepared outline or to listen to the speech given by another student. The position to be taken in the speech disagreed with the initial position of both speaker and listener. Change-scores indicated that speech-givers changed more in the direction of the discrepant position upheld by the speech than did listeners and that those speech-givers who showed the most change were those who had engaged in the greatest improvisation in their talks and who were more satisfied with their performances.

A second study (King & Janis, 1956) was designed to gather evidence on the separate effects of improvisation and satisfaction in producing change of opinion. Again each student was given a speech upholding a position discrepant from his private opinion. In the first group he was asked to read the speech silently, in the second to read it aloud, and in the third to read it silently and then give it aloud as would an impromptu speaker. Questionnaires showed that subjects who gave the improvised speech were less satisfied with their performance than were those who simply read the speech aloud. If improvisation increases attitude change, the group that improvised should show more change, whereas if satisfaction increases change, the group that merely read aloud should show more change. The results showed a greater percentage of subjects changing toward the position upheld in the speech in the group that improvised. There was no difference in the amount of change between the group that read the speech aloud and the control group that read the speech silently.

A more recent study by Culbertson (1957) asked subjects who held negative attitudes toward Negroes either to play or to watch being played the role of a Negro who is moving into a previously all-white neighborhood. It was found that control subjects were least likely to change their attitudes to become more favorable toward Negroes, observers next most likely, and role-players most apt to show favorable attitude change.

While the general reasons for attitude change and its general direction can now be understood, what, according to the dissonance formulation, controls just how much tension a person experiences? Or, to put it more rigorously, what are the factors controlling the amount of dissonance created and therefore the amount of consequent attitude change? To answer this question, we must consider one of the central assumptions of the theory, that the magnitude of dissonance is a direct function of the proportion of dissonant to consonant cognitions among all relevant cognitions. The greater the number of cognitions consonant with engaging in discrepant behavior, the less the dissonance upon engaging in it; the fewer the cognitions consistent with engaging in discrepant behavior, the greater the dissonance. Thus, the greater the ratio of dissonant to consonant cognitions, the greater the dissonance and the greater the attitude change toward the originally unacceptable position. Translated into simpler terms, the more compelling the reasons for doing what goes against your values, the less the dissonance; the fewer the supports for doing it, the greater the dissonance, the greater the pressure to reduce it and, having engaged in the behavior, the greater the change of attitude so as to reduce it. Making one's attitudes consistent with the discrepant behavior one has engaged in makes it no longer discrepant; there is no longer any conflict between what one believes and what one has done, and one is restored to a state of psychological comfort.

The Effects of Rewards or Incentives

Common sense tells us that a man will say anything, without necessarily believing it, if he is threatened with punishment for not saying it; a confession to any crime can be produced if the coercion is strong enough. But what will induce a man to change his beliefs? Dissonance theory, by invoking its proposition about the ratio of dissonant to consonant cognitions, says that the greater the number or importance, or both, of the cognitions consonant with agreeing to engage in disagreeable behavior, the less the dissonance. What this proposition means is that the fewer the incentives used to produce commitment, beyond those necessary to get the person to comply, the greater the dissonance and the greater the change of attitude. Thus, large rewards can always serve as a rationalization for having done something objectionable; with only small rewards, the person must find a solution internally, and one way he can rationalize his behavior is to bring his attitudes into line with his behavior so that he no longer experiences dissonance. Thus, the concept of dissonance leads to the paradoxical position that the *more* reward you get for engaging in a discrepant act, the *less* you actually change your attitudes in the direction of believing the worth of the position you took; the less reward, the more change.

This proposition was first tested experimentally by Kelman (1953); though he did not frame his research in terms of dissonance, the results seem to be well accounted for by dissonance theory. He offered different rewards to junior high school students if they would write essays in support of a comic book they disfavored (for younger children's reading). Under one set of conditions, writing in support of the disfavored book meant giving up a moderately attractive prize for a small chance of getting a highly attractive prize, whereas for another group, it meant getting both moderately and highly attractive prizes and giving up nothing. Attitude change was measured by asking the subjects to indicate, both before and after writing the essays, how good or bad they considered each of twelve different comic books, representing both favored and disfavored types.

Those subjects who wrote in support of the initially disfavored book showed the effects of counterattitudinal persuasion. Change-scores showed that their attitudes became more favorable toward the initially disfavored book. In addition, the subjects who received low rewards and had to compete for them showed greater favorable change than those who were eligible for high rewards. It is thus apparent that, at least under the experimental conditions stipulated, a person induced to argue against his private attitude will tend to change his attitude toward the position for which he has argued. Furthermore, the lower the rewards offered, the greater the amount of change in the direction of the discrepant position. Both a large reward and the certainty of getting it are compelling reasons for compliance and consequently produce less dissonance and less change of attitude.

An experiment by Festinger and Carlsmith (1959) which stemmed specifically from the assumptions of dissonance theory bears also on this issue. They required college students to perform a boring and tedious task and then asked each to tell the "next subject" that the task was interesting and enjoyable. For making this false statement some subjects were offered $1 and others $20. All subjects were then interviewed in order to measure their evaluation of the boring and tedious task about which they had made the false statements. To ascertain that the task was really unpleasant, a third group was interviewed after it had performed the task without having been asked to make a discrepant statement. It was assumed that dissonance aroused by making the statement discrepant with one's private evaluation of the task would produce a more positive evaluation of the task. The results for the three groups confirmed the assumptions that: (1) the task was unpleasant; (2) making a statement discrepant with one's true evaluation tends to produce change in evaluation toward the position of the statement; and (3) the amount of change in evaluation decreases as the amount of money offered for the discrepant statement increases. The results thus confirm the theoretical expectations.

These data on the effects of rewards for behavior discrepant with beliefs are in the main consistent with dissonance theory. The inverse relationship between rewards and attitude change might, however, disappear if the rewards were small enough. If the inverse relationship obtained is due to the fact that large rewards engender suspicion and resistance, subjects would react by saying to themselves something like, "It must be bad if they're paying me so much for it," and the fact that subjects who are rewarded highly show less change than subjects who receive lower rewards could be due, then, to this kind of resistance. Therefore, it could be argued, if sufficiently small rewards are given, suspicion and resistance will be reduced and the relationship between reward and attitude change will be a direct function of the amount of money paid to the person for taking the discrepant stand. In order to check this point, Cohen (see Brehm & Cohen, 1962, pp. 73-78) carried out an experiment in which rewards were varied at intervals over a wide range. The variation was accomplished by offering college students either $.50, $1, $5, or $10 to write an essay taking a stand against their private views on a current issue on campus. Under the guise of a "general survey," students were asked to write an essay "in favor of the actions of the police." This issue was chosen because, just before the study, there had been a students' "riot" at the college and there had been resulting accusations of police brutality toward students. The results of the experiment are entirely consistent with the notion that dissonance and consequent attitude change vary inversely with the amount of payment for taking a stand discrepant with one's cognitions. As the reward decreased, attitudes toward the police became more positive: those who received $.50 changed most, those who received $1 changed next most, and so on. The fact that the results show a consistent inverse relationship between reward and attitude change over a wide range of rewards supports the derivation from dissonance theory that a decrease in cognitions consistent with discrepant commitment (less reward) increases dissonance and consequent attitude change.

The Effects of Justification

The analysis of reasons for and against discrepant behavior suggested by the theory of dissonance applies not only to rewards and material advantages but also to justifications of all sorts for engaging in discrepant behavior. A number of investigators have studied the justifications for carrying out discrepant behavior: Cohen, Brehm, and Fleming, 1958; Rabbie, Brehm, and Cohen, 1959; and Brock and Blackwood, 1962.

The first set of investigators asked college students, in a classroom setting, to write an essay supporting the side opposite their private view on an issue of current campus interest. Under the guise of a survey for the university administration, the second group of investigators asked college students to write essays supporting the elimination of intercollegiate athletics (earlier tests had shown that most students were strongly against elimination). The third set of investigators asked students to write essays against their own private opinions on the issue of higher tuition. In all three experiments half the subjects were given, in order to create low dissonance, a series of reasons for writing the discrepant essay—it would help science, help the experimenter, be valuable to the school administration, and so forth; to create high dissonance, the other half were given minimal reasons.

The outcomes show identical trends: the groups given low justification became more positive toward the originally discrepant attitude than the groups given high justification. The data from all three experiments clearly show that dissonance and consequent attitude change are related to weaker and less compelling reasons for performing or participating in an act which is not consistent with one's values or loyalties.

The Effects of Coercion

Just as large rewards, material benefits, and justifications can produce discrepant behavior, but not necessarily true attitude change, so can strong threats and coercions. Since threats of punishment, like rewards, are reasons for doing something one does not want to do, the more strongly they are invoked, the more the person may be willing to support the discrepant stand, but the less dissonance he will experience and the less his true attitude will change. Thus, the less the coercion, beyond the minimum necessary to obtain compliance, the greater the dissonance and the greater the consequent attitude change. In effect, under these conditions the individual becomes a willing collaborator in persuading himself; in this manner he reduces the dissonance occasioned by behaving in a manner following from the obverse of his cognitions.

This proposition was tested in an experiment by Brehm (see Brehm & Cohen, 1962, pp. 84-88). Brehm predicted that where there was less coercion, the subjects would like a boring and time-consuming task better after committing themselves to it. His aim was to make the subjects choose to perform the unpleasant task by threatening them with differing amounts of punishment.

The experiment was conducted with pledges for a fraternity. The experimenter (a fraternity member) explained to each pledge that he was taking a course in psychology in which he had to collect some research data. His project, he said, was to get normative data on the copying of random numbers. What he wanted the pledge to do was to copy random numbers for a three-hour stretch. He admitted that participation would not be fun, that it would indeed be boring and tedious, but he insisted that he had to get it done.

The manipulation of coercion was introduced by telling half of the subjects (low coercion) that if they did not sign up for the experiment they would be paddled, and by telling the other half (high coercion) that they would be called before a tribunal or even kept out of the fraternity if they did not sign up. After the subjects had agreed to participate, their attitudes toward the task were measured. It was found that satisfaction with the task increased as the magnitude of the coercive force decreased. This study, then, supports the hypothesis that dissonance increases as the magnitude of the coercive force to comply decreases (provided that compliance is obtained) and confirms the proposition that increasing the number or importance of cognitions, or both, supporting a discrepant commitment produces less dissonance and less attitude change.

A study by Aronson and Carlsmith (1963) is the mirror image of Brehm's. Just as Brehm decreased the coercion to perform something unpleasant and found that liking increased, Aronson and Carlsmith decreased the coercion to withdraw from an attractive object and thus produced increased dislike. They were concerned with the degree to which the coercion used to force the rejection of a desirable alternative would produce attitude change regarding that alternative. Their subjects were nursery-school children who were asked which toy they would like to play with.

Half of the children were given a mild admonition not to play with the toy, which was put on the table (mild threat); the other half were strongly admonished not to play with the toy on the table under threat of the experimenter's anger, annoyance, and rejection of the child (strong threat). The experimenter then left the room. The children were then allowed to play with other toys; later the experimenter returned and the children reranked all the toys in the room. Aronson and Carlsmith expected that the children, having committed themselves to the discrepant behavior of not playing with something they found desirable, would experience greater dissonance the fewer the cognitions supporting the discrepant commitment. Severe threat is a cognition more consistent with giving up a desirable object than is a mild threat. Thus, the subjects who had been threatened mildly would experience greater dissonance and could reduce it by evaluating the crucial toy more negatively than those who had been threatened severely. The results strongly support the hypothesis; the children who refrained from playing with the toy when only mildly threatened reduced the dissonance between not playing with the toy and the cognition that it was attractive by derogating the toy.

However we look at coercion, the more we are forced to do something we dislike doing, the less dissonance we feel over doing it. If what we dislike is to approach something unpleasant or to avoid something pleasant, we experience dissonance to the extent that the coercions forcing such discrepant acts are minimal. The weaker the coercions, the less reason there is for doing the undesirable thing, and the greater the dissonance. The greater the dissonance, the greater change in attitude. If one has approached something bad, one has to like it in order to reduce dissonance; if one has stayed away from something good, one learns to dislike it in order to make one's cognitions consistent.

Characteristics of the Person Who Induces Compliance

In addition to material benefits, rewards, justifications, and coercions as factors affecting dissonance, there is the agent who compels the discrepant behavior. This person, too, can obviously be regarded as a reason for or against agreeing to comply, and thus his role is also susceptible of analysis in terms of the ratio of dissonant to consonant cognitions. An attractive, pleasant, decent, warm person can generally get us to do what he wants us to do; if we do something unpleasant because he asks us to, we should experience little dissonance, for his admirable traits are compelling reasons for doing it. On the other hand, there are fewer compelling reasons for performing some disliked act for someone who is nasty, envious, cold, and cruel, and if for some reason we do, we should experience greater dissonance and thus greater attitude change toward the discrepant position we have upheld.

Thus we arrive at a paradoxical prediction: the more disliked or negative the inducing agent, the more dissonance, and consequently the more change of attitude toward an unpleasant or discrepant position. Such a prediction seems not to follow from common sense, but it can be explained by dissonance theory, and it was tested by Smith (1961). In his experiment, the subjects were Army reservists. They were given a preparatory questionnaire which included an attitude scale on their liking for grasshoppers as a food. Then the experimenter, who was introduced as an Army researcher, acted in a friendly, warm, permissive manner toward half the subjects throughout the experimental period. He smiled frequently, referred to himself by a nickname, sat on the counter, told the subjects to smoke if they wished, said that they should relax and enjoy themselves. Toward the other half of the subjects the experimenter acted throughout in a formal, cool, official manner. The men were ordered rather then requested to follow instructions; they were told that they could not smoke; the experimenter never smiled; he stood in a stiff pose and replied in a sharp manner to all questions.

After both groups of subjects had been induced as part of the "research" to eat at least one grasshopper (encouraged by the offer of fifty cents), they filled out the attitude measure again. When the change-scores were examined, the subjects toward whom the experimenter had been cool showed more increase in liking for grasshoppers than those toward whom he had been friendly. Thus, the more negative the characteristics of the inducing agent, the fewer the cognitions supporting commitment and the greater the dissonance. Having once engaged in the behavior, one can reduce dissonance by changing one's attitude to be more consistent with it.

Characteristics of the Person Committing Himself

Another approach to specifying the reasons for and against discrepant compliance as a key to understanding attitude change in such situations is to look inside the person who complies, at the motives and characteristics which more or less compel him to do so. High self-esteem, for example, is a cognition that does not support compliance; the person of high self-esteem is accustomed to think of himself as having integrity and of his opinions as correct and true. A person with low self-esteem has characteristically been shaken in his convictions and has had his opinions questioned; when induced to adopt a discrepant stand, he should experience less dissonance and consequently less attitude change. We might expect, therefore, that the higher the self-esteem, the more the dissonance upon complying and the stronger the pressure on the person to reduce those tensions, everything else being equal, by justifying his stand more and by being more certain that his new position is the correct one. In general, any personality trait that would lead a person not to perform a discrepant act contrary to his initial attitudes will produce more dissonance and consequently greater attempts at the reduction of dissonance when he does perform it.

In an experiment by Gerard (1961a), subjects were first convinced that they were either high or low in the ability to make accurate judgments about a series of perceptual stimuli. They were then placed in a situation in which the objectively correct response to a set of perceptual stimuli was quite clear, but where two other persons gave unanimous but frequently incorrect responses. An electrode was then placed on the forearm of each subject, and he was told that it measured the implicit movement of his muscle. In this way the subject was led to believe that his "first impulse" for each of the next series of judgments would automatically register on a signal panel in front of him and on signal panels in front of two other subjects who were to judge the same stimuli. He found, according to the signal panel, that his first impulse was either to conform to others' judgments regardless of whether or not they were correct or to make the correct choice regardless of others' responses. In short, the subject was led to believe that he was a conformer or a deviate after having received information that he was either high or low in the ability to make similar kinds of judgments.

The subject who "conforms" can reduce the dissonance between his "behavior" and his cognitions about himself by increasing the attractiveness of the group to which he has presumably "conformed." Furthermore, we should expect that the higher his ability, the greater the dissonance over having "conformed" and the greater the consequent attraction. The results showed that subjects whose ability had been rated high experienced more dissonance on compliance than subjects of low ability, and in order to reduce that dissonance (make consistent their cognitions about their ability and their compliance) they became more attracted to the group and modified their behavior in the direction of the group's on a subsequent series of trials.

Choice in Compliance

In a sense, all these determinants of the attitudinal effects of forced compliance can be subsumed under a more general factor: the extent to which the person feels that the situation is putting pressure on him to comply. To the degree that he thinks it is, whether through rewards, justifications, or coercions, he feels little dissonance and changes his attitude less; to the degree that he thinks it is not, even though he complies, he feels greater dissonance and consequently changes his attitude more. In sum, the question is the degree of *choice* a person experiences in engaging in discrepant behavior in situations of forced compliance. A number of experiments have attacked this question directly.

Suppose, for example, that an investigator wishes to induce a subject to support an opinion different from what he privately believes, where the alternative is to uphold his true position. The investigator might establish a condition of low choice by telling the subject that he has been assigned by chance to support one position or the other. Some of the attributes specifically associated with the position that the subject is supposed to take are that choosing that side will please the experimenter and help science, or that refusing to choose it means no participation at all (and the subject has volunteered to participate). A high degree of choice, on the other hand, might be induced by telling the subject that he may support the opposing side, but that he does not really have to, and that it is completely up to him whether or not he does. (The subject is, however, induced to take the opposing side just as in the condition of low choice.) With high choice, there is the implication that the subject will still be helping the experimenter and science no matter which side he chooses—though his taking the side opposite to his private belief will be more helpful.

The direct manipulation of choice was first used by Cohen, Terry, and Jones (1959) in the experiment mentioned in the preceding chapter, where subjects chose to expose themselves to communications contrary to their actual positions. Davis and Jones (1960) also manipulated choice. They induced dissonance by having college students make unnecessarily derogatory remarks to a person who was presumably a student being evaluated on several personality dimensions. All of the subjects were informed that this "student" was to hear either a positive or a negative evaluation, but some were told that they had been assigned to give one of the two kinds of evaluation according to whether they were odd-numbered or even-numbered subjects, while others were told that they could give either a positive or a negative evaluation but that what was really needed was a negative evaluation. Later the subjects rated the person whom they had evaluated falsely; subjects who had been given a high degree of choice rated him more negatively than did those who had been given little choice. Seeing a person more negatively makes one's negative behavior toward him consonant. Thus, dissonance and consequent attitude change toward a discrepant stand increase with choice in taking that stand.

Experiments by Brock (1962), Brock and Buss (1962), and Cohen and Latané (see Brehm & Cohen, 1962, pp. 88-91) also provide evidence of the effect of choice on dissonance and consequent attitude change. Brock had non-Catholic subjects write essays in favor of becoming a Catholic; Brock and Buss induced subjects who were on record as being opposed to the use of electric shock in experiments to give others electric shock; Cohen and Latané induced students who were against the introduction of a compulsory course in religion to make tape-recorded speeches in favor of such a course. In all three experiments, half of the subjects were given high choice in engaging in the discrepant behavior and half of the subjects were given little choice. The data in all three experiments show that subjects given high choice changed their attitudes more than subjects given low choice toward agreement with the discrepant act or stand. In general, the data support the assumption that variations in choice in taking a stand discrepant from one's attitudes produce variations in attitudinal change toward that discrepant position; the greater the choice, the greater the change of attitude.

Not only is choice directly relevant in producing attitude change immediately; the effects of negative events which occur in a situation long after compliance has been achieved are also dependent upon the degree to which the person has had choice in complying originally (Brehm, 1959; Brehm & Cohen, 1959). The question Brehm was trying to answer was: Does a negative occurrence arouse dissonance if it occurs after a choice has been made? He had junior high school students eat a small dish of a vegetable they disliked in order to obtain a prize. To see whether or not a further inconsistent cognition would increase the magnitude of dissonance occasioned by eating the vegetable, the experimenter told some of the subjects, when they had nearly finished eating, that he intended to write a letter to their parents telling what vegetable they had eaten. The implication was that the subjects would then be expected to eat the vegetable at home; the letter constituted an additional event inconsistent with the commitment to eat the vegetable and was outside the control of the subject. Dissonance arising from having had to eat the vegetable could easily be reduced by increasing liking. If being told about the letter created additional dissonance, then these subjects should show a greater increase in liking for the vegetable than those who were not told about the letter. The expectation was clearly supported by the results.

This experiment suggests that a person need not know about a factor at the time of choice in order to experience dissonance when he does learn of it. Thus, exposure to information inconsistent with a prior commitment will sometimes create dissonance. It should be noted, however, that the commitment in the present study (having eaten the disliked vegetable) occurred through the subject's own choice. He was not forced to eat; he chose to eat.

Another study (Brehm & Cohen, 1959) confirms the hypothesis that inconsistent events can create dissonance even when they are due to chance, but shows that they do so only to the extent that the individual feels he has had a choice earlier in undertaking a discrepant act or commitment.

The results of these experiments involving choice all show that attitude change supporting an inconsistent commitment increases as the degree of choice in making the commitment increases. Thus they have many implications for situations where people try to change other people's attitudes by forcing them to do something they do not want to do. Not only are they relevant to purposes which are invidious, like thought control or indoctrination, but they are also important for desirable ends like instituting progressive public policy. In achieving successful desegregation, for example, policymakers who place constraints upon people to get them to comply with a situation they do not like should take into account the desirability of their perceiving a certain amount of choice in complying if attitude change is to be maximally effective. In effect, public policy is probably most effective when it makes the best possible compromise between the forces necessary to obtain compliance and the person's own feelings of choice in compliance.

Amount of Discrepant Behavior

Greater activity in behalf of something one dislikes should create greater dissonance. In effect, the more effort put into taking a discrepant position—the more ingenious the arguments given in its favor, the longer one engages in it, the greater the sincerity and willingness to do a good job of it—then the greater the dissonance when it is inconsistent with one's attitudes, and consequently the greater attitude change toward favoring it. In an experiment carried out by Aronson and Mills (1959), the experimenters induced dissonance in female college students by requiring them to take an "embarrassment" test in order to join a discussion group on sex for which they had volunteered. To produce low dissonance, the subject was required to read a list of sex-related words to the male experimenter. To produce high dissonance, the subject was required to read a list of obscene words to the same experimenter. After the test the subject was allowed to audit a supposed group discussion, which was actually tape-recorded and which was designed to be dull and uninteresting. Finally, the subjects were asked to indicate how good they thought the discussion and how much they liked the members of the group.

Having favorable attitudes toward the discussion and toward the group constitute cognitions consistent with joining the group; hence, dissonance created by engaging in the embarrassing test in order to get into the group can be reduced by increased favorable attitudes toward the discussion and the group members. The more embarrassing or painful the test required in order to get into the group, the greater the dissonance created and the more favorable should be the attitude. The results confirmed this hypothesis.

Brock and Buss (1962) showed that attitude change is determined by the *amount* of painful shock subjects had to give. Their study examined the effects when subjects chose to deliver shock although they were on record as opposing such punishment. The stronger the shock they give, the greater should be the dissonance and consequently the tendency to reduce dissonance. Dissonance in this situation can be reduced by evaluating the stimulus as less noxious—by saying, in effect, "The pain I administered was really rather mild." Thus, a main hypothesis of the study was: the greater the intensity of the shock delivered, the greater the minimizing of its painfulness. For the subjects who were given a choice in how much shock to deliver, the greater the magnitude of shock they delivered, the greater the dissonance and consequent minimizing of the painfulness of shock. Thus attitudes, whether toward social groups or toward subjective experiences, will change more the more of the discrepant behavior the person engages in.

Confrontation by Discrepant Behavior

What are the effects on attitude change of being publicly confronted with the products of one's discrepant behavior in a social situation? A clue to the answer is provided by the experiment in which Brock (1962) had non-Catholic subjects write essays supporting Catholicism under conditions of high and low choice in compliance. Within each of these conditions, however, he confronted half of the subjects with the request that they analyze their discrepant essays in terms of the meaning and implications of their discrepant position. The other half were asked to deal with their discrepant essays by focusing on the grammatical structure. In this manner the subjects might be said to have been differentially exposed to the implications of their discrepant acts. His results show that, for those who had been given high choice originally, the more they were exposed (the more their attention and thinking were focused on the implications of their discrepant stand), the greater the attitude change. Thus, when dissonance occurs through choosing to engage in discrepant behavior, its effects and thus attitude change are enhanced when the person is exposed to his discrepant product.

The foregoing applications of the theory of dissonance show that this model is a powerful tool for understanding the attitudinal effects of discrepant behavior and often illuminates paradoxical and obscure consequences of such behavior. Its central hypothesis stresses the importance of the ratio of dissonant to consonant cognitions—the supports for and against adopting a discrepant stand. Thus, where there are small rewards, few material benefits, few justifications, little coercion, much choice, high self-esteem, an unpleasant inducing agent, and strong discrepant behavior, dissonance will be greatest and attitudes will change most toward favoring the discrepant position to which one is committed. Conversely, it will generally be true that, with other factors held constant, the greater the number or importance, or both, of consonant cognitions associated with the alternative chosen, the less the dissonance resulting from a choice to engage in discrepant behavior. As we have seen, this proposition has been tested by a variety of studies designed specifically for that purpose. The common characteristic of these studies is that they have induced a person to make a statement or to perform an act which is inconsistent with what he privately believes or feels. Thereafter, one way in which he can reduce the resulting dissonance is by changing his attitudes so that they more nearly coincide with what he has said or done. Change in the person's private belief or evaluation has therefore been taken as evidence for the existence of dissonance, and it has further been assumed that the greater the change, the greater the dissonance preceding the change.

The theory of cognitive dissonance therefore allows us to understand and analyze the effects of enforced discrepant commitment. It provides information about: (1) the sources of inconsistency, or what factors arouse motivation to reduce inconsistency; (2) what factors make for more or less attitude change; and (3) why and when inconsistency produces attitude change—how inconsistency affects the person experiencing it.

7

THE INFLUENCE
OF THE GROUP

To THIS POINT we have been examining the processes and determinants of attitude change from an individual standpoint; the discussion has dealt with external appeals directed toward a person and with that person's response according to his cognitive and emotional make-up. People do not, however, exist in isolation, and their thoughts, attitudes, and actions are inextricably interwoven with those of the other people around them. We are all members of one group or many, no matter how fleeting, amorphous, and informal or how stable and organized these groups may be. In all our daily activities, we take positions, arrive at decisions, and carry out actions against a backdrop of other people with whom we are involved in a network of responsibility and mutual regard. Family, friends, classmates, teammates, instructors, counselors—these and many others constitute reference points for us, and our opinions and actions are partly shaped by them. The present chapter examines the means by which social groups influence the attitudes and behavior of their members.

Our day-to-day concern with our own actions and thoughts often causes us to lose sight of the implications of being immersed in a social world. All our lives, whatever we have done and learned and continue to do and learn is carried out within the context of involvement with others. Over the past two decades, social scientists have become more and more aware of the intimate relationship between a person's thoughts and actions and the social matrix in which he exists. From his earliest years an individual's relationship to others is one in which he perceives them as aiding or frustrating his needs, and the very language the child learns from his interaction with others around him enables him to differentiate himself from the world and to elicit responses from others. Finally, every person depends upon others for his view of the world around him, for his standards of right and wrong, and for the establishment of his ideals and aspirations. Thus we are all part and parcel of the social world about us; for human beings, social reality is an ever-present determinant of behavior.

When we consider this intimate relationship between the person and the social group, we can understand how breaking up a person's stable relationship with the group about him can be an effective precursor to influencing him. The very reasons that make the group important to him for establishing a stable view of himself and the world around him make for all sorts of effects of the group upon his behavior. Because a person is so completely interdependent with others, disrupting the relationship creates chaos within him and makes him vulnerable; because it is therefore so important to him to maintain a close and stable relationship with others, those others can influence his behavior in a variety of ways.

The present chapter first takes up the degree to which decisions made within a social group affect an individual's later attitudes and behavior. Then it explores some of the psychological processes underlying the individual's reliance on groups of which he is a member and some of the consequences of his reliance for change in individual attitudes and opinions. Finally, it traces the processes by which influence is exerted from person to person by examining the networks of communication which connect persons of different social groups or different positions within a group to one another. An examination of these aspects of social influence should provide a reasonably good overview of the ways in which influence is exerted within a group and the forms such influence takes in shaping an individual's attitudes and behavior.

Group Decision

What implications do decisions made within a group have for behavior outside the group? Much of the civic and community activity undertaken in our society is based on the assumption that groups can mobilize individual activity. Everyone knows that getting an entire community or group organized to do something, aside from being more efficient than individual solicitation, is often more effective. Why this should be true is not yet entirely clear. Some answers to the question come from a pioneering study of group influence carried out during World War II by Lewin and his associates (1943), who studied the effect of group decision on the attitudes and behavior of members of a group toward strongly held, traditional food preferences. Their aim was to change the consumption patterns of housewives from food which they ordinarily ate to meats which they usually bypassed, like beef hearts, kidneys, and sweetbreads. The housewives were organized into groups and exposed to two different experimental treatments. To some of the groups, a lecturer gave a compelling talk on the nutritiousness of these meats and their relative economy, and gave possible recipes for their preparation. To the other groups, exactly the same information was given, but in the form of a discussion in which the housewives took an active part. Following the discussion in the latter groups, the housewives were asked to indicate by a show of hands whether they intended to serve the unfamiliar meats. When all of the housewives were again questioned some time after the experiment, it was found that they differed considerably: more of the women from the groups where they had made individual decisions in the group setting after discussion were serving the unfamiliar meats (32 per cent) than were the housewives from the groups which had heard the lecture (3 per cent).

In another study, the same investigators used as subjects farm women who had just had a first child in a nearby state hospital.

Before they were discharged from the hospital, the mothers received information about the value of feeding their new babies cod-liver oil and orange juice. Usually the new mothers received such information individually from a nutritionist connected with the hospital. In order to test the efficacy of this traditional practice against a group procedure, Lewin and his students arranged mothers into groups of six so that they could receive the same information in the form of a group discussion. When the discussion was over, the mothers were asked to state publicly whether or not they intended to give their children orange juice and cod-liver oil. In follow-up studies made two and four weeks later, the method of group decision was shown to be far more effective than the lecture method in leading to the actual use of cod-liver oil and orange juice.

These early studies indicate that the greater effectiveness of group decision in changing attitudes and behavior is related to the fact that the individual acts as a "group member" rather than wholly in terms of his personal preference. They do not, however, identify the specific factor or factors which make the difference—lecture or discussion, decision or no decision, degree of consensus arrived at in the group, degree of publicity attached to the decision.

A study by Bennett (1955) attempts to distinguish the relative contributions of various factors. In her experiment she attempted to increase the willingness of undergraduates in an introductory psychology course to volunteer as subjects for experiments. She divided the students into a number of groups: some groups made no decision, some made decisions with varying degrees of individual anonymity, some discussed the material, some heard lectures about it, and finally some served as control groups. The various combinations of the factors of group discussions, decision, degree of public commitment, and degree of consensus reached by the group permitted an assessment of their differential importance in determining behavior governing volunteering.

The results show that group discussion is not necessarily more effective than a lecture in influencing group decision, nor is greater public commitment more effective than less public commitment in assuring that the decision will be carried out. *The act of making a decision* and *the degree of group consensus* perceived by the individual, taken together, appear to account for the effectiveness of group decision in influencing action. Thus, how the decision is related to future action is important, and a high degree of consensus on a new decision is effective in increasing the probability that it will be carried out.

Bennett's conclusion that group discussion is not especially effective in itself has, however, been questioned by other investigators (Pennington, Haravey, & Bass, 1958). They found that opinions changed more when discussion was allowed than when it was not, and although they found that decision-making was of some importance, it did not appear to play so large a role as the discussion itself. Although these findings appear to contradict Bennett's, an examination of the experimental conditions shows that whereas Bennett's subjects were asked to make an individual decision in a group setting, the subjects used by Pennington and his associates were asked to come to a consensus as a group. Thus it appears that for individual decisions it makes no difference whether people receive a lecture or participate in a group discussion. So long as they perceive some consensus in the group within which they make personal decisions, there will be some effect on their future action. On the other hand, when the consensus of an entire group, as a group, is sought, a discussion seems to be more effective than a mere lecture. Before a group of people can come to a consensus, in other words, they need a feeling of participation and a chance to consider alternatives together; a lecture may not serve the purpose. Additional support for the importance of discussion alone under some circumstances comes from an experiment by Mitnick and McGinnies (1958) in which group discussion was found to have greater long-term effectiveness in changing attitudes than did lectures.

It seems clear, then, that group decision serves to motivate the members of a group to work on a group task and to accept a goal established by the group as their own personal goal. Although many factors may contribute to the effectiveness of group decision, one of them is evidently consensus. When there is unanimity or near-unanimity in a group, its members adopt the desired actions more readily than when no such unanimity exists. Group decision may be effective, then, because it trades on the pressures in a group toward conformity to group norms; these pressures can help to bring about adherence to a new norm the group has adopted. The ramifications of conformity and deviation within social groups are thus likely to have implications for understanding how social influence is exerted.

Conformity and Deviation

When the supports for an individual's beliefs, attitudes, and values are removed through his isolation and separation from his group and through the undermining of his friendships, he is prevented from validating them through meaningful interaction with others. Recognition of the need to validate one's beliefs and to see oneself and one's world through the eyes of others provides a basis for understanding the pervasive effect of social interaction on a person's attitudes. The following section examines the psychological processes involved in the intimate relationship between the individual and the group.

The situation where an individual's actions in face-to-face contact with others place pressures on him to judge, believe, or act in concert with them (to accept their influence) is popularly termed "conformity." Conformity has been a favorite topic of denunciation by everyone from college presidents in commencement-day speeches to disaffected toilers in the vineyards of Madison Avenue. The use of the term for purposes of research, however, requires clarification of some of the surplus meanings associated with it.

First of all, the mere fact that people do things in concert with others does not constitute conformity; the nature of social life is such that we inevitably rely on others for information, opinions, and advice, particularly in the absence of clear and unequivocal signposts for behavior. Many kinds of behavior which appear conformity are simply manifestations of the process of arriving at consensual validation of a new standard or a fact of social life. In effect, much that is frequently called conformity is necessary in the daily course of social life. At the other extreme, however, are people behaving in response to pressures exerted by others, whether the pressures are actual or are merely felt as pressures by the particular person. Conformity is sometimes produced by a desire to be in step, since being out of step may imply loss of status or identification as abnormal. Here, too, however, we have learned from the history of our behavior vis-à-vis others that being peculiar or different has consequences for the receipt of rewards or punishments. Thus there are "reasons" why people submit to the pressures placed upon them by social forces even when the physical world presents clear and unambiguous alternatives. In a sense, then, everyone both does and does not "conform," and to speak of conformity as an invariant, invidious state is to oversimplify the task of specifying the conditions under which people behave more or less under the influence of others. Everyone will "conform" under some conditions; the problem for investigation is to determine the group, situational, and personality factors making for more or less acceptance of influence from others around us. The unsolicited acceptance of influence for reasons of status seems closest to conventional definitions of conformity; at the other extreme, reliance on others in ambiguous situations seems less like what is generally meant by conformity.

The distinction, an important one, is thus between need for status and need for information. Social influence may be accepted either to the degree that it evokes the desire of the individual to improve or maintain his status vis-à-vis others or to the degree that it involves his dependence upon others for information about himself and the world around him; of course, there is an entire range of gradations between these extremes, as well as various combinations of the two sets of factors. The first set of motives for acceding to the group we may call "normative" or "motivational" determinants; the second set are "informational" or "uncertainty" determinants. In the normative situation, the person's self-picture is reflected against others and against the rewards and punishments he may gain from them. In the informational situation, the person accepts others as sources of influence because he uses them as stable sources of information for evaluating the world around him. These factors interact, but they can be separated into distinct processes for purposes of analysis. Fuller treatments of these issues are to be found in Berg and Bass (1961) and Walker and Heyns (1962).

Some Classic Experiments

An individual is seated at a small table in a dark room. He sees a tiny stimulus light through a small hole in a metal box placed at the front of the room. He is told to watch the light at the signal "Ready" and that after a short time he will see it move. As soon as he sees it move he is to press a key which will make the light disappear. The experimenter then asks the subject to tell how far the light moved and to try to make his estimates as accurate as possible.

This situation utilizes what is known to psychologists as the autokinetic effect, an effect which depends upon the fact that where there is complete darkness, as in a closed room or outdoors when there is no moon, a single small point of light appears to move erratically in all directions. Thus it is possible to present an objectively stable stimulus which cannot be definitely localized because there is nothing in reference to which one can locate it. The fact offers an opportunity for the study of group influence: the conditions can be structured in several ways according to the character of subjectively established points of reference.

Under the experimental conditions described above, the subject is asked to stop after 100 judgments. The data show that after some widely varying judgments, he has established a range and an extent, and a point (a standard or norm) within the range which is peculiar to himself. This subjectively established standard or norm serves as a point of reference with which each successive experienced movement is compared and judged to be short, long, or medium within the subject's own established range. Thus, when the person judges an autokinetic stimulus by itself, his behavior reflects a general psychological tendency to experience things in relation to a frame of reference.

Sherif (1935), who designed the experiment described, carried this finding and this technique over into group processes in order to investigate the operation of influence upon the individual in a group situation. The questions he asked were: "How will the individual in a group perceive the stimulus field?" "Will the group affect his judgments and will he carry these effects over into a situation in which he subsequently faces the stimulus without others around him?" To answer these questions, Sherif investigated some subjects first as individuals and then in groups. Other subjects received the reverse treatment: they started in group sessions and ended in individual sessions.

The results show that when an individual who has developed his own range and norm is put into a group with other individuals who have developed their own ranges and norms, the ranges and norms tend to converge. The convergence is not so great, however, as when all of them first work as a group, since individuals have had less opportunity to set up their own stable norms. When as members of a group people face the same unstructured, unstable situation for the first time, they set up a range and standard peculiar to the group, and when they subsequently face the same situation as individuals, they perceive it in terms of the range and standard that they bring from the group.

This experiment illustrates the formation of a social norm in a laboratory situation and shows some of the psychological bases of social norms. When stimulus situations are unstable in their physical characteristics, they allow internal or social factors to dominate the way in which they are perceived. Thus all of us face new stimulus situations with certain modes or standards or frames of reference which have been built up within the context of a social group. And, in fact, such established social norms as stereotypes, fashions, fads, and customs are all partly the product of shared frames of reference built up through contact between individuals. Once such norms are established, they determine the way in which people will face subsequent situations—social and nonsocial alike. Here, then, is one of the reasons underlying the acceptance of influence: people influence each other in setting a common norm or frame of reference which each of them then uses as a standard for perceiving the world. One clear function of influence is thus to help an individual use the standards of the group in an ambiguous situation, in order to facilitate his adjustment to that situation when he faces it later alone. If subjects can be influenced to adopt a prescribed or predetermined set of ranges and norms and these norms can take the form of evaluative predispositions when there is no stable frame of reference for evaluating objects, attitudes can be shaped and formed within the context of the social group.

A very different kind of experimental manipulation of group factors was carried out by Asch (1951). Imagine a person sitting at a table with eight others, all of whom have volunteered to take part in an experiment which involves the discrimination of length of lines. The group is told that their task is to match a standard line with one of three lines differing in length, and that, since the number of lines is few and the group small, each person will be called upon in turn to announce his judgment. Our subject occupies a seat near the end of the row so that he gives his judgment seventh, following most of the group. Since the sizes of the lines used as stimuli are clearly identifiable, it comes as a surprise to the subject in question that some of the other persons present begin after a while to make "incorrect" judgments. He is even more shocked to discover shortly that everyone is making a judgment he feels to be incorrect. For perhaps the first time in his life he is faced with a situation in which a group unanimously contradicts the evidence of his senses. When his turn comes, what will he say? On the answer to this question turn a number of significant issues in the analysis of social influence.

Asch's experiment concerned some of the social and individual conditions that induce individuals to resist or to yield to "group pressures" when they are perceived as contrary to fact. To this end, Asch arranged a situation in which the individual is placed under group pressure which can be systematically manipulated and controlled; the individual can then be measured in terms of his readiness or tendency to respond to the pressure. Thus, in the situation described, the individual's opposition to the group was made dramatic by having every other person present a confederate of the experimenter; they had been instructed beforehand to give unanimously incorrect responses on certain of the judgments of the length of the lines. The one naïve subject therefore found himself in a situation full of conflict, where correct answers would be in opposition to those given by a unanimous majority. What should he say? Who will agree with the group and who will not? What sort of characteristics typify conformers and what sort of characteristics typify those who remain independent? Most important, what conditions will produce more or less conformity or more or less independence? These questions all constitute major problems for research, and a large body of evidence has been accumulated in an effort to answer them.

Asch's experiments themselves provide tentative answers to some of these questions. Although most of the naïve subjects remained independent throughout the experiments, a substantial minority (about 40 per cent) yielded to the group and modified their judgments in accordance with those of the majority. The degree of independence or yielding was a joint function of the stimulus (the unclearness of the stimulus, the closeness of the three reference lines to each other), the character of the group forces (the degree to which the opposition was unanimous and the size of the group in opposition), and the character of the individual (there were wide differences between individuals under the same experimental conditions). These answers are stated as generalities; they do not define explicitly the underlying psychological bases of conformity, but they represent a starting point from which most of the more recent research has been launched.

Sherif's and Asch's experiments represent important, even classic, contributions to the study of social influence. They differ in that Sherif mainly exploits the individual's need for a stable reference point in an ambiguous situation, while Asch exploits his needs to conform to the expectations of others. Both experiments no doubt contain elements of both processes, but they seem clearly to revolve around different determinants of social influence. More recent research on social influence has generally attempted to separate these different sources of influence and to show that they do, indeed, have their own unique psychological bases and their special consequences for conformity. A study by Deutsch and Gerard (1955) illustrates these two bases of influence in a single experiment and serves as an important bridge between these pioneering studies and later research on the conditions under which more or less influence occurs.

The investigators define normative social influence as an influence to conform to the positive expectations of others; informational social influence they define as an influence to accept information contributed by others as evidence of reality. Commonly, they say, these two types of influence are found together, but they are separable: it is possible to say things which one disbelieves, but which agree with the beliefs of others, in order to conform to the expectations of others, and it is possible to accept someone else's beliefs as evidence of reality even though one does not have a specific motivation to conform to his expectations. In their experiment, they set up three main conditions: a face-to-face situation much like Asch's; an anonymous situation in which the subjects were separated by partitions and indicated their judgments by pressing a button; and a group situation in which the subjects were separated physically but were given instructions about performing well *as a group* in order to win a prize. Within these conditions, some subjects were divided into those who committed themselves privately to their judgments by writing them down, others who committed themselves privately, but could erase their judgments, and still others who committed themselves publicly, since they knew that their judgments were to be handed to the experimenter.

In an experiment of this kind, the major measure of conformity is the number of errors the subject makes which are in the direction of the predetermined errors made by the "group." The results of the experiment show that subjects who believed that they were members of a group made more errors (conformed more) than those who did not participate in the task as members of a group. This result illustrates normative social influence, where the expectations of others are important insofar as subjects think they are cooperating in order to win a prize. Conversely, when the individual feels that his judgment cannot be identified (when he remains anonymous), normative social influence is reduced: the subjects conform less, since there is less chance for them to be identified as violating the expectations of the group and therefore to be deprived of social rewards. Fur-

thermore, when people commit themselves to their own judgments either publicly or privately, normative social influence is
also reduced; commitment to one's own judgment results in
less conformity to the judgments of the group. Finally, the more
uncertain the person is about the correctness of his own judgment, the more likely he is to be susceptible to social influences
in making his judgment.

These results indicate that when groups are created for a
given purpose, normative social influence increases as people
strive to conform to the expectations of the group. When normative social influence is removed through anonymity, conformity declines; there is presumably less motivation to conform to
others' expectations when one cannot be punished for deviation. Even with anonymity, however, there is more conformity
to the judgments of others than in a control situation where subjects make their judgments alone. In the absence of normative
expectations, the effect may be due to dependence upon the
judgments of others insofar as they are seen as trustworthy
sources of information about the objective reality with which
the subject is confronted. The more ambiguous the objective
reality, of course, the more conformity as the person uses others
as stable points of reference (see, for example, Kelley & Lamb,
1957).

A good deal of what we ordinarily refer to invidiously as conformity thus appears to be related to the judgments of others as
factors to be weighed in making one's own judgments. To the
degree that we see other people as motivated and competent to
judge accurately, we use them as bases for our own judgments.
Our entire experience of socialization teaches us that the perceptions and judgments of others are often reliable sources of
evidence about reality. Hence, as Deutsch and Gerard point out,
if the judgments of two or more people in the same objective
situation are discrepant, each tends to re-examine both views
to see if they can be reconciled. This process resembles that of
referring to a computing machine for support. Except in the
most indirect sense, these processes can hardly be termed normative, or tending toward what we usually call conformity;
rather, they are informational.

Much of the research involving so-called conformity can be

interpreted as the investigation of informational social influence. This not to say that normative influence is ever entirely absent from any social situation. It does mean, however, that the less salient the social group, the fewer normative influences it produces and the less it arouses processes related to the expectations of others, which is what we ordinarily refer to as conformity. When normative social influences are increased through the creation of a group with specific norms, standards, and goals, the role of informational influence becomes smaller and the role of normative expectations in producing conformity becomes greater.

In considering informational versus normative social influence, the major motive affecting the acceptance of informational influence appears to be the reduction of uncertainty. A person who holds an opinion different from that of others tries to get the others to agree with him in order to reduce his uncertainty. One of the major determinants of uncertainty, and thus of the acceptance of informational social influence, is therefore the amount of ability a person feels he has for making the requisite judgment. Ability, then, may be one of the major bases for making direct social comparisons: in order to reduce uncertainty, a person feels a need to supplement his own ability. Numerous experiments concerned with social influence (see, for example, Gerard, 1954; 1961a) are consistent with this view and illustrate how differences in ability, in situations of uncertainty, can lead to social influence.

Processes of Social Comparison

An attempt to build a general psychological theory of social influence based on informational and normative components is Festinger's (1954) theory of social comparison processes. This theory deals with the appraisal and evaluation of abilities and opinions, and provides a framework for understanding how attitudes are changed through social influence. Festinger begins with the basic assumption that there exists in the human organism a drive to evaluate his abilities and opinions. People use objective, nonsocial means to evaluate their opinions and abilities, but where these are not available, people evaluate their abilities and opinions by comparison with the abilities and opinions of others. Where there are no opportunities for either physical or social comparison, the person's subjective evaluations of his abilities and opinions are unstable.

So far as opinions are concerned, a person is likely to choose for comparison someone whose opinion is close to his own, provided that there is a range of possible persons for comparison. When the only social comparison available is a very divergent one, the person is not able to make a subjectively precise evaluation of his opinion, and instability results. In this situation, since subjective evaluations of opinions are stable when others have similar opinions and unstable when others' opinions are different, the person will experience pressures to change his attitudes toward those of others. Also, given this need for a stable self-evaluation, a person will be less attracted to situations in which others are very divergent from him in opinions. The existence of differing opinions in a group is thus likely to lead to action by the members to reduce the discrepancy, thereby producing attitude change. Since opinions are so strongly based on social definition, there are few objective restraints to opinion change and one can change one's opinions so as to be closer to others'. A result is that a discrepancy produces tendencies both to change one's own position so as to move closer to others in the group and to change others in the group so as to move them closer to oneself. In this way attitudes change within the context of dependence upon others for a stable evaluation of the world and oneself. The person changes his attitude to be close to others when he has to depend upon them for definition of the social world.

Normative influences are relevant, also, since any factors which increase the strength of the drive to evaluate a particular opinion or increase the importance of a particular comparison group will increase the pressure toward uniformity concerning that opinion. Thus, the stronger the attraction of the person to the group, and the greater the relevance of the opinion to the functioning of the group, the stronger the pressures toward uniformity of opinion. While attitude change is related to the use of the group as a standard of reference, it is thus true that normative considerations also enter to determine attitude change in the direction of conformity with others who are group members.

Several investigators have examined the operation of normative factors in this context (Emerson, 1954; Hochbaum, 1954; Schachter, 1951). They have shown that there are serious negative consequences of not adhering to the standards of a social group in which there are strong pressures toward uniformity. In their studies, deviates in such groups are rejected by other group members. If a person desires to maintain his membership in a group, therefore, and to attain status, recognition, and acceptance, he must change his attitudes to meet the group's standards. These normative factors are important in determining the effectiveness of social influence, and become operative to the degree that the norms and standards of behavior of attractive groups are made salient for the individual. From this point of view, any action which the individual can take in the direction of changing his attitudes toward the group is an overture to maintaining or improving status. This process is what is popularly termed "conformity"; the mainspring of attitude change here is the desire of the individual to be close to others so that he will gain the social rewards of being close to them and avoid the social punishments attendant upon being out of line. These motives sometimes lead the individual, in situations where his senses tell him one thing, to say that he sees or believes something else, and to deny publicly the authenticity of his own immediate experiences and judgment of the social world.

Much of the research on social influence deals with normative processes of social comparison which depend on expectations of social reinforcement (status, recognition, acceptance) from others. The experiments aim at the specification of the conditions under which persons who are making judgments within a group context do in fact conform to the judgments of others. Some of the factors which have been isolated are *situational,* like the size of the group, its composition, the degree to which consensus within it approaches unanimity, the intensity with which the group holds its consensus, the strength of the coercion it applies, the atmosphere of the larger social environment, and the possibility of feedback about whether one has been right or wrong. Some factors relate to *individual differences in tendencies toward conformity*—one's past experience, one's sex, one's social status. Still others are *personality factors,* such as a person's cognitive and emotional make-up, his self-concept, the quality of his interpersonal relations, and his personal attitudes and values.

A fuller discussion of these factors and their significance may be found in Krech, Crutchfield, and Ballachey (1962). Here it is sufficient to note that in considering normatively determined conformity we must also consider the individual's predisposition toward emotional dependence upon others in his group. Taking all of the above-mentioned factors into account leads to the conclusion that people who tend to accept social influence readily in situations where physical stimuli are relatively clear are those whom we would call conformers by the broadest social definition; they may be characterized summarily as people who have learned at an early age to conform in order to reduce social fear and anxiety. They seem to need more social approval from others, to be more fearful of stepping out of line, to have a greater need for affiliation with others, and in general to be more dependent on others and fearful of rejection by them. Learned anxiety and fear reduction may thus be the primary mechanism of normative social influence; the tension associated with disagreement with others decreases when one resolves that disagreement by changing one's attitudes so as to conform to the group's position.

Patterns of Social Influence

Now that we have examined some of the factors affecting the acceptance of influence within social groups, we may look at the channels through which this influence flows. In *The People's Choice,* Lazarsfeld, Berelson, and Gaudet (1948) reported a study of Erie County, Pennsylvania, in the 1944 election. Their study made use of the panel technique, in which measurements of attitudes and of exposure to communications are obtained during repeated interviews with the same persons over a period of weeks or months.

The investigators found that radio, newspapers, leaflets, and similar media had only a slight influence on voting; what influenced people most was other people—friends, family, community contacts. It is these "opinion leaders" who serve as mediators between communications from the mass media and other people; they are attuned to the appeals current in the mass media and in turn interpret those appeals to the members of their social groups. Thus ideas flow from television, radio, and the printed page to opinion leaders, and from them to less active segments of the population.

This hypothesis has come to be known as the "two-step flow of communication" (Katz, 1957). It reflects that aspect of interpersonal relations which has implications for understanding channels of communication and is consistent with the view that interpersonal relations are sources both of social pressure and of social support. This concept of the flow of influence was further developed and extended in a study of election behavior in Elmira, New York, in 1948 (Berelson, Lazarsfeld, & McPhee, 1954).

Early studies implicitly assumed that in a "mass society" informal communications played a minor role. These more recent studies emphasize the role of informal personal influence and must be considered against the background of the research on group influence and the importance of measures of connections between persons within a given group. The result has been that stress on the importance of the mass media in producing attitude change has decreased, and emphasis has shifted to the importance of personal influence in understanding how attitudes are shaped and changed in our complex society.

An investigation of influence and opinion leaders carried out in Decatur, Illinois, reflects this trend (see Katz & Lazarsfeld, 1955). The study dealt with the flow of influence in respect of public affairs, marketing, fashions, and moviegoing. The respondents were asked by the investigators to name the persons they believed to know most about things in general, the persons they considered to be most trustworthy, the persons who had actually influenced them in determining some specific change, and the persons with whom they most often talked over what they learned from newspapers, radio, magazines, and other sources. In order to reconstruct the patterns of influence, the interviewers followed up a considerable sample of the names that respondents gave them, and even followed up some names given to them by the persons first named.

The Decatur study showed that the subject matter being transmitted is important in determining who will lead and who will follow. In marketing, for example, opinion leadership is concentrated among older women with large families, whereas for moviegoing and fashions, it is the younger, unmarried girl whose advice is sought. Yet within these categories, people were found, by and large, to talk most of all to others like themselves. Only in public affairs was there some concentration of leadership among those of the highest status. Influence appears to be related to who one is, to what one knows, and to where one is located. The person who accepts influence may want to be like the opinion leader because the latter personifies certain values. He turns to those whom he deems more competent in a given area and to those who are accessible—to the persons he knows, who themselves may know others outside the group. Opinion leaders show more exposure to the media in the sphere in which they have influenced, and also, in some spheres, are more affected by the media in making their own decisions. In other spheres, opinion leaders report personal influence as the major factor in their own decisions, suggesting the presence of longer chains of person-to-person influence. It is possible to demonstrate that opinion leaders are distributed widely throughout society, that they may be different persons for different areas of opinion, and that they read more than nonleaders.

Along these lines, Menzel and Katz (1955) carried out a study of the adoption of new products and the diffusion of information by physicians. They interviewed almost all of the physicians in a given community, examined records of their prescriptions, and established sociometric patterns among them (the colleagues they saw most often socially, the colleagues with whom they talked most frequently, and the colleagues to whom they looked for information and advice). It was found that a doctor's decision to adopt a drug early or late after its appearance is mostly determined by his integration into the medical community: the more frequently he is named by colleagues as a friend or discussion partner, the more likely he is to be an innovator with respect to a new drug. Extent of integration seems to be a more important factor than age, medical school, income of patients, or readership of medical journals. Doctors who are more in touch with other doctors are apparently more up-to-date, and doctors who feel integrated have more social support and feel more secure about facing the risks of innovation. Furthermore, it was found that doctors were likely to prescribe the same drugs as their friends and colleagues and that they tended to adopt new drugs at virtually the same time, especially when they were confronted with new and puzzling cases—a clear reflection of the operation of informational social influence. Some mass media serve to "inform" the doctors, other media to "legitimize" their decisions; professional sources of information such as colleagues play a legitimizing role, while commercial media play more of an informative role.

The doctors who were influential were more likely to be readers of a large number of professional journals and to value them more highly than doctors of lesser influence. They were also more frequent in their attendance at out-of-town professional meetings and maintained contact with a greater diversity of medical institutions and societies. Opinion leaders, then, serve to relate their groups to important facets of their environment through whatever media are appropriate, whether they be medical journals or scientific meetings. The pervasiveness of personal influence in mediating the effects of mass media is indicated by the fact that about 50 per cent of the members of each medical clique who adopt a new drug do so within a few days of one another and by the fact that, except for the pioneer, no physician who adopts a new drug does so unless he has direct contact with a doctor who has already used it.

It is clear, then, that persuasive communications stemming from the mass media and from authoritative communicators are not by themselves a sufficient condition for producing attitude change; they function instead through a nexus of mediating factors and influences like individual predispositions, selective perception, selective exposure, interpersonal relations, group pressures, and personal influence (see Klapper, 1960). These factors generally render mass communications a contributory agent rather than the sole cause of attitude change; the effects of the mass media must be understood in terms of the psychological and group factors through which they pass.

8

ATTITUDINAL INOCULATION AND IMMUNIZATION

IN CONSIDERING the problem of resistance to attitude change, all the factors assumed to be related to decreasing the acceptance of influence are relevant. Thus, if the reverse of everything we have seen to be productive of attitude change were invoked (high self-esteem instead of low, unreliable instead of credible communicators, and so forth), we should expect greater resistance to attempts at persuasion. Such an approach, however, would be merely a static invocation of processes studied in the context of what makes for more change. In analyzing actual resistance to change, it is essential to examine evidence specifically gathered to bear upon resistance; resistance may not be a mere mirror image of acceptance, and the explicit study of how it is built up may highlight novel phenomena in the whole field of attitude change.

How is it possible to build up people's resistance to possible assaults on their beliefs? An analogy may be made with the way the body becomes immunized against a disease if it encounters a mild enough form of the disease beforehand; to what degree are people immunized against arguments if they experience a mild form of those arguments beforehand?

In the experimental work on the effects of one-sided versus two-sided communications (see Ch. 1), a question was raised about the role of the two-sided communication in preparing people to meet subsequent counterarguments. An experiment by Janis, Lumsdaine, and Gladstone (1951) illustrates inoculation in its most general form: their results showed that people who had been given a previous communication about the great problems involved at the end of the war in constructing and testing an atomic bomb were much less inclined than a control group to believe that the Russians would soon have large numbers of A-bombs after their explosion of one. Thus preparatory communications can be effective in reducing the impact of subsequent information.

From similar experiments the general principle of inoculation has emerged in some detail. The analogy to the medical situation is clear: just as we develop the resistance to disease of a person raised in a germ-free environment by pre-exposing him to a weakened form of a virus so as to stimulate, without overcoming, his defenses, so also we can develop the resistance to persuasion of a person raised in an "ideologically clean" environment by pre-exposing him to weakened forms of counterarguments or to some other belief-threatening material strong enough to stimulate, but not so strong as to overcome, his defenses against belief (see McGuire & Papageorgis, 1962).

This reasoning assumes that if there is no threatening stimulation, the person will not be sufficiently motivated to learn the defensive material. His general tendency to avoid dissonant information may have made him overconfident of the strength of his belief and thus not much motivated to seek out further defensive material. Thus, the inoculation argument runs, a "supportive" defense which gives a person only positive reasons for maintaining his attitude will seem obvious to him, and he will not learn enough to provide much immunity to later, unexpected assaults.

Janis has made an interesting application of these principles to the study of surgical patients (see Janis, 1958). He believes that authoritative preparatory communications about impending stressful events such as surgery serve a number of functions. First of all, they counteract a person's tendency to discount the potential danger and thus modify his attitude of complete invulnerability. Anticipatory fear, thus created by realistic information, leads to the development of reality-based defenses against fright. Secondly, preparatory communications supplement the person's spontaneous protective measures by teaching him what he can do to ward off or minimize the danger and by showing him what reassurances he can count on for reducing his fear when he is actually in the threatening situation. Finally, they facilitate reliance on experts, authorities, and family and friends.

Janis emphasizes the importance of the proper *dosage* of fear-arousing stimuli; he notes the superior effectiveness of moderate as against strong fear-appeals and concludes that the individual's threshold for the arousal of fear or anxiety will determine the degree to which he will be influenced by a communication making severe threats (see Janis & Feshbach, 1953). Thus doses of fear in the middle ranges would seem to be most effective. Too small a dose does not serve to stimulate defenses, too large a dose brings diminishing returns as psychological resistance increases and acceptance decreases.

Janis' application of the principle of inoculation to emotional and fear-arousing stimuli highlights the psychodynamic processes and psychological changes that can affect successful inoculation. His results, however, provide relatively little information about how to prepare and deliver communications which will achieve such changes or how they relate to the issue of attitude change in general. A series of experiments by Mc-Guire and his co-worker Papageorgis, undertaken largely at the University of Illinois' Communications Research Center, represent an attempt to carry the investigation further—to specify a number of empirical principles which govern the conditions under which one kind of preparatory communication or another will facilitate resistance to change.

McGuire and Papageorgis (1961) set out to determine the relative effectiveness of various types of prior defenses in making a person's beliefs resistant to persuasion when he is later forced to expose himself to massive doses of counterarguments. They began with the assumption that people tend to defend their beliefs by avoiding exposure to contradictory information, especially in the case of noncontroversial cultural truisms, and that for this reason these untried beliefs prove highly vulnerable to persuasion in situations of forced exposure. Since people tend to be unmotivated to develop a defense of their beliefs to the extent that they consider them invulnerable, the researchers felt that they could most effectively immunize a person against persuasion by pre-exposing him to arguments supporting the belief. They also hypothesized, however, that since the person is unpracticed and unmotivated in defending the belief, the pretreatment will only be effective provided that the person is not overly active in the defense and participates in it under guidance.

(It should be noted that other investigators have seriously questioned the invariance of the tendency to expose oneself only to supportive communications. There are probably some conditions which induce people to seek supportive information and other conditions which create a susceptibility to adverse information; in any case, a great deal of additional research is needed before firm conclusions on this question can be reached. See Steiner, 1962.)

McGuire and Papageorgis told college freshmen that they were participating in a study of verbal skills. In a first session they received defenses of (statements supporting) various truisms about health and health practices. The experimenters then exposed half of the subjects to statements which consisted of counterarguments and explicit refutations of those arguments; the other half were exposed to arguments supporting their beliefs. Within each of these groups, half the subjects wrote an essay supporting their beliefs and the other half read such an essay. Finally, within each of the four subgroups, subjects were divided into passive and active readers and guided and unguided writers. After receiving these different treatments, the subjects' attitudes were measured to test the direct strengthening effects of the communications. In the second session, the subjects were then exposed to strong counterarguments regarding beliefs some of which had been defended and some of which had not. In order to gauge the comparative immunizing effects of the several types of defense, the subjects' final beliefs were measured after exposure to the strong counterarguments.

The results showed that beliefs were influenced in the absence of immunizing counterarguments. Furthermore, the refutational defense conferred more resistance than the supportive one. On the other hand, the effect of immunization in protecting beliefs decreased progressively as active participation in the defense increased: reading the defense provided more resistance to the second set of counterarguments than writing it.

Following up these results, the experimenters performed a second experiment (Papageorgis & McGuire, 1961). On the basis of the finding that weakened counterarguments confer more resistance to persuasion than supportive arguments, they suspected a generalized immunization effect. Thus, through prior defenses, a person would be resistant to strong doses not only of the specific counterarguments refuted but of alternative counterarguments against the belief as well. They assumed that the generalized effect would result, through pre-exposure, from the person's having been stimulated to think up supporting arguments for his belief and from his discounting the credibility of later attacks on his belief.

The major hypothesis of this experiment was confirmed. The refutational defense produced resistance to later novel counterarguments as well as to the counterarguments which had originally been refuted. The generalized effect of prior defense was shown to be related to a feeling on the part of the subjects that the counterarguments were not credible. Finally, the immunized subjects thought up more arguments and arguments of better quality in support of their original beliefs than did the nonimmunized subjects.

Delving deeper into the complex interrelationships between the factors involved in resistance to persuasion, McGuire combined the perspectives of the first two experiments into a third one (McGuire, 1961a) which showed that a passive defense is superior to an active defense in developing resistances to attacks by familiar counterarguments, but that an active defense is superior in protecting the person against novel counterarguments. He found also that a double defense, both active and passive, is superior to either one alone in developing resistance when the same counterarguments as were refuted earlier are used in the later attack.

The reasoning behind these experiments rests on the assumption that people characteristically defend their beliefs by avoiding exposure to discrepant information, especially in the case of cultural truisms where discrepant information is rarely available. This position, as has been noted, leads to overconfidence about one's beliefs and to little motivation for assimilating supportive material. McGuire (1961b) investigated these assumptions directly in an experiment in which he dealt explicitly with supportive material. He reasoned that when a person's belief is threatened in the course of a defensive session, his motivation for using supportive materials increases and he becomes more resistant to subsequent persuasion. Thus, while the supportive defense by itself may not be of use in increasing resistance, it may be of value in conferring resistance when it is used in combination with refutational defenses.

From this experiment, McGuire concluded that supportive arguments have a good deal of value. They may be more effective than refutational arguments when given alone insofar as increasing resistance to new information is concerned, and they may be very effective when given in conjunction with refutational defenses. The results of this experiment provide strong support for the notion that refutational defenses which mildly threaten belief by merely mentioning and refuting counterarguments against it motivate the subject to assimilate supportive material. The supportive material, once assimilated, becomes a potent force in increasing resistance to later persuasion.

In a more recent experiment, McGuire and Papageorgis (1962) explicitly tested the notion that prior defenses confer resistance against later attack only when a truism is threatened (a subject is little motivated to assimilate material in support of a truism he feels is invulnerable). The feeling of threat was manipulated by announcing to half of the subjects that they would first read defenses of their beliefs and then attacks on them. The other half were not forewarned and were led to think that the experiment was a test of verbal skills. The investigators expected that the immunizing effect of all the defenses would be enhanced by the warning, but that, more importantly, the supportive defenses would gain more from it than the refutational defenses.

The results indicated that forewarning did indeed confer more general resistance against a later attack than no forewarning, leading to the conclusion that since refutational defenses contain an intrinsically provocative element (counterarguments), they need less of the further motivational stimulation conveyed by forewarning. That motivational stimulation is necessary for supportive defense is consistent with McGuire's major argument that a subject must feel that a truism has been threatened before he can assimilate supportive material as an aid to increasing his resistance.

All of the studies in this series tested the effectiveness of prior defenses without reference to the time interval between defense and attack. If our understanding of these issues is to be thorough, we must know something about the lasting effects of immunization, of how long it can continue to increase resistance to persuasive attempts. McGuire (1962) attacked this problem in another, related experiment and found again that defenses conferred resistance to immediate attacks, but that the resistance conferred by supportive defenses fell off more rapidly than the resistance provided by refutational defenses. In fact, the difference in effect was so striking that no appreciable resistance remained from supportive argument two days afterward, whereas resistance was found one full week after a refutational defense. Also, resistance to the counterarguments explicitly refuted fell off more rapidly than resistance to novel counterarguments; most surprising of all, there was greater resistance to novel counterarguments two days after a refutational defense than immediately after it.

These interrelated experiments on resistance to attitude change serve to enlarge our picture of attitude change as a whole (see also Manis & Blake, 1963). A number of cautions should, however, be kept in mind in interpreting and generalizing the results of the research. For one thing, and for various theoretical reasons, the studies were confined to cultural truisms in which the believer's confidence was initially high. With issues that are more controversial, different results might follow. A person is more aware that controversial beliefs are subject to attack and is more highly motivated to assimilate supportive defenses, even without forewarning. Secondly, a refutational defense might, in the case of a controversial issue, elicit an avoidance response because of the ambiguous, somewhat threatening initial content, especially when the person is forewarned of an attack on his beliefs. Many of the effects that have been described might therefore be reduced, or even conceivably reversed, as one goes from cultural truisms to controversial issues.

More generally, a number of questions about the process of inoculation still demand answers. Would different issues and different methods of experimenting with them yield different results? What about lengthening or shortening the interval between defense and attack? Would more subtle measures of attitude show different results? These questions are, of course, relevant to every piece of empirical research that has been mentioned throughout this book. With special reference to inoculation, as we pursue the medical analogy, we might ask: "How thoroughly weakened should counterarguments be before a person is pre-exposed to them?" "What dosage achieves maximal immunity with least danger?" "Do small doses of weakened counterarguments, given repeatedly, have more effect in producing resistance than one massive dose?" "If so, what is the most efficacious spacing of the doses?"

While the formulation of a general theory of immunization awaits answers to these questions, the fact remains that McGuire's program of research has illuminated a number of significant determinants of resistance to persuasion. Like any good research endeavor, it raises more questions than it answers. When we consider the constant bombardment almost all of us receive from the mass media, we see the importance of this kind of research. By examining a number of factors underlying the process of immunization, these investigators have given us a number of practical aids for the stimulation of critical thinking in the face of the attempts at indoctrination and the wholesale attitudinal merchandising that pervade our society. While it is true that their research was confined to cultural truisms and did not touch controversial issues, enough of our daily lives revolves around such truisms to make the research significant.

9

CONCLUSION

Experiments versus Surveys

Because of our concentration on the psychological factors involved in attitude change, we have depended almost entirely on evidence gathered in the psychological laboratory by means of controlled experimental research; we have largely neglected the survey as a tool for research on communication and attitude. Surveys, which are carried out by means of large-scale interviewing of respondents chosen through random sampling of a population, deal with the distributional, ecological, socioeconomic, and social-group determinants of attitude change rather than with the psychodynamics underlying change. They do, however, present a picture of attitude change somewhat different from the one that emerges from a scrutiny of the experimental data. Hovland (1959) and Lipset and his associates (1954) have discussed this problem in detail.

Experiments and surveys differ in their approaches to attitude change. In the experiment, as we have seen, individuals are given a controlled exposure to a communication and the effects are measured in terms of the amount of change in attitude or opinion; in the survey, information obtained through interviews or questionnaires concerns both the respondent's exposure to various communications and his attitudes and opinions on various issues. In addition, surveys sample different segments of the population and are carried out in the natural environment, procedures rarely employed in experimental research. Surveys are thus able to give their results wider generality than most experiments can, but it is more difficult for surveys to give definitive answers to problems because of their lack of control over causal relationships.

The picture of the effects of persuasive communications that has emerged from correlational surveys indicates that few individuals are ever affected by communications. Research using experimental techniques, on the other hand, indicates the possibility of considerable modification of attitudes through exposure to communications. The difference in outcome of the two methods can be accounted for by differences in research design and by traditional differences in the general approach of the two kinds of investigator.

In experiments, the effects of exposure are gauged on the whole range of individuals being studied; in surveys, only on those who choose to expose themselves to the communication—those who are in general already in favor of the communication. The people who are most influenced in the laboratory are therefore those who in the natural setting do not expose themselves to influence; the result is that the effects are exaggerated in the controlled experiment as compared with the survey.

The differences in general approach include the following:

1. In surveys, the unit to be evaluated is usually an entire program of communication, while in experimental studies the focus is on some specific variation in the content of the communications or the personality of the recipients, and experimental evaluations usually involve single communications.

2. The time interval used in evaluation is different. In the experiment, the effects are usually observed immediately or soon after exposure to the communication; in the survey, the time perspective is much more remote. Since effects sometimes decline with time, the net outcome is accentuated in experimental, compared with survey, studies.

3. Experimental studies generally utilize communicators who are teachers, and experiments are often carried out in school or college classrooms. This setting lends an authority, a high de-

gree of motivation or incentive, and great deal of credibility to the experimental situation, thereby making for attitude change. The survey uses remote individuals as communicators; they are outsiders who are often known to espouse a point of view different from that held by the respondent.

4. Surveys usually reach the person in his natural environment, with the consequence that there are supplementary effects produced by discussion with friends and family. Such discussion, which is usually absent in artificially constructed laboratory situations, often serves to bring people back to the group positions from which they may have strayed as a result of the persuasive communication.

5. The survey is designed to sample randomly the entire population or a broad segment of it; the typical experiment uses college students because they are more accessible.

6. Experiments generally study a set of factors or conditions which are expected on the basis of theory to influence attitude. Toward this end, experimenters try to find issues involving attitudes susceptible of modification through persuasive communications. Otherwise there are likely to be no measurable effects, especially since the experiments are on a small scale. Surveys typically deal with socially significant attitudes which are more deeply rooted and to which people are more highly committed.

These differences in approach have important consequences for an understanding of the factors underlying attitude change, as two examples will show. Since experimental studies deal with issues which are relatively less involving and where expert opinion is highly involving, opinions may be considerably affected by persuasive communications, and the advocacy of a position considerably discrepant from an individual's own position may lead to a substantial change of attitude. Experimental evidence on the effects of the credibility of the communicator (see Ch. 2) supports this generalization. On the other hand, since surveys usually utilize issues which are basic and involve deep commitment, little change of attitude would be expected, and the more discrepant the individual's position from the communication, the less he might change; he might, in fact, even strengthen his original position (see, for instance, Freedman, 1961).

Investigation of the efficacy of different orders of presentation (see Ch. 1) shows that primacy is not invariably predominant and that there are many conditions under which recency will operate. In experiments, the audience is often systematically exposed to both sides of an issue, or different communicators may present opposing views successively, or the setting of the presentation may make clear that the points of view are controversial. All these factors work in the direction of reducing the effects of primacy. Surveys, on the other hand, have produced the widely adopted generalization that primacy is an extremely important factor in persuasion, especially in political and commercial propaganda. This result probably stems from the fact that in surveys the advantage of the first side is not only that it is the first, but that it is often the only side of the issue to which the audience is exposed. Once they have been influenced, many persons make up their minds and are no longer interested in other communications on the same issue.

The generalizations, then, about the role of certain crucial psychological processes underlying attitude change depend upon whether one resorts to the survey method or to the experimental method. Inferences about the relationship between discrepant communications and attitude change or about the role of primacy and recency may be quite different, depending on whether the data come from a laboratory experiment or from a survey.

Examples of Methodological Integration

There is, however, no necessary contradiction between survey and experimental approaches; their divergent results can be accounted for by differences in research design and different characteristics of the situation. The experimenters are becoming increasingly aware of the narrowness of the laboratory setting for investigating the larger, more interconnected effects of communication, and the research workers making surveys are coming to realize the limitations of the correlational method where experimental control of exposure is not possible.

Some studies have attempted to take advantage of both types of design. A study by Deutsch and Collins (1951) aimed at determining the effect on the attitudes of whites toward Negroes of living in interracial housing projects. They arranged detailed interviews with a sample of housewives in each of four housing projects, two segregated and two integrated. The results, which were amplified and replicated in a later study by Wilner, Walkley, and Cook (1955), showed that the white occupants of the integrated housing projects were likely to have more positive attitudes toward Negroes and to have more contacts with them than those who lived in segregated projects.

This kind of study uses an *ex post facto* design. While not strictly an experiment, it uses a design in which effects are traced backward to certain causal factors assumed to have operated at a previous time. By using procedures which rely on selective control, the design attempts to identify these causal factors by currently available measures. In Deutsch and Collins' study, the problem was to interpret the results so as to ascertain the most valid causal factors responsible for them. The authors' hypothesis is that the experience of living in an integrated housing project and interacting with Negroes (presumably under favorable conditions of contact) produces a favorable change in the attitude and later behavior of whites toward Negroes. They present a great deal of control evidence which argues against another possible interpretation, that the two types of projects selected individuals who were initially different in their attitudes toward Negroes. The authors bolster their argument by showing that the occupants of the projects did not differ in initial attitude, although they may have differed in a number of other characteristics. To establish this point, they made several different comparisons of the occupants of the integrated and segregated projects; these comparisons were assumed to be relevant to the prediction of attitude change in the housing situation. Thus, retrospective questions concerning initial prejudice were asked; lengths of stay of the respondents in the two kinds of project were compared; checks were made of different motives for moving into the project; comparisons were made of attitudes toward Negroes in general and toward Negroes in the project; and respondents from different projects were compared on the basis of social and political characteristics that are often associated with prejudice. No matter what kind of comparison was made, occupants of the integrated housing projects showed less prejudice toward Negroes. All this is taken by the authors as evidence that, regardless of the original composition of the projects, occupants of the integrated projects had become less prejudiced than occupants of the segregated ones. Thus, though it was impossible to carry out an experimental test of the contact hypothesis, the authors applied a number of retrospective controls to their data in order to make causal inferences, at the same time doing justice to the complexity of attitude change in a real-life setting.

Another approach to the integration of experimental and survey methodologies is the quasi-experimental study—Hyman and Sheatsley, 1947; Scott, 1956. This type of design represents an attempt by investigators making surveys to control the stimuli presented to the respondent. Direct reports of (1) the experimenter's operations in introducing the issues in which he is interested and (2) the reactions of respondents who have been exposed to these operations may provide evidence of the existence of major determining factors. The result is greater precision in interpreting effects of various kinds. The quasi-experimental study is an improvement over the traditional survey, which simply picks up responses where they exist and tries to infer causal sequences from an analysis of what may have happened in the environment. In general, social scientists have to make the best possible compromise between the rigor gained by experimental control and the social significance of problems pursued in real settings. These more controlled surveys represent a desirable trend in research.

Problems for Research

What else ought we to know in order to arrive at maximal understanding of the determinants of attitude change and social influence? One could answer "Everything," in view of the amount of conflicting information and the large gaps in our knowledge of the processes of attitude change. Social scientists have only just begun to put together the knowledge derived from studies using different methodologies and stemming from different theoretical biases. Considering the complexity of the task and the newness of the venture, they have made a good start. Much as we still need to know, however, what appear to be the most strategic next steps in research on attitude change and social influence? What information would be of most value to begin to fill in the picture?

The Internalization of Attitude Change

A critical issue in the understanding of attitude change is the degree to which outer conformity to persuasive appeals is transformed into inner change, and the conditions under which this transformation will occur. People can very often accede overtly to the demands of authoritative communicators or to the strictures of their social groups without necessarily undergoing any inner transformation. The problem is still little understood, but there are hints toward understanding the conditions under which internalization occurs. Both Kelman's (1961) research and the dissonance formulation (see Chs. 5 and 6) deal with the problem of internalization; while Kelman's model lays out a number of categories under which one or another kind of attitudinal response (public or private change) takes place, the dissonance formulation adds to it a more microscopic analysis of the actual cognitive conditions under which internalization results. Juxtaposing these two models provides us a framework which is helpful in carrying out further systematic analyses of the implications of internalization for communication.

Social Judgment and Attitude Change

The intimate relationship between the understanding of attitude change and progress in basic psychological theory can be seen by examining research on the higher learning processes, especially in the areas of perception and judgment. Most of the experiments we have considered make many implicit assumptions about the way in which people react to attitude scaling. Since their reactions affect their answers and, in turn, the inferences we draw about change and its determinants, we need to know more about the degree to which the response an individual gives is affected by his attitudinal anchorage point, about the effect of distance between his position and that of the communicator, and about the degree to which issues are important to him. A major start in studying these problems has been made by Manis (1960), Sherif and Hovland (1961), and Upshaw (1962).

Conflict and Attitude Change

A large body of psychological thought (see Miller, 1944; Miller, 1959) concerns the major types of psychological conflict and their consequences for apathy, withdrawal, loss of interest, aggression, and related responses. Persuasive communications may arouse conflicts between an individual's original motives for holding a given attitude and the motives aroused by the new incentives offered by the communication. Sometimes a single communication arouses two incompatible motives, as in the case of two-sided communications; at other times the initial reactions to the source and to the content may be incompatible. Understanding of the outcome of attempts at changing attitudes could be increased by examining the theory relating to different kinds of conflict. Some beginnings have been made toward analyzing persuasion in terms of conflict (Janis, in Hovland, 1957, pp. 170-186; Weiss, 1953).

Attitudinal Persistence and Decay

Another important problem for research is assessment of the retention of attitude change and the duration of its effects. Some progress in understanding the factors determining how long a change will persist and the factors producing decay has already been made by Hovland, Janis, and Kelley (1953). As they have shown, certain delayed attitudinal effects can be explained by the absence of the original communicator as a cue for acceptance or rejection, leading to a splitting of source from content so that those who originally changed most show a considerable loss, while those who changed less may show an increment. Reminding the person of the source tends to prolong the change over time. While it is clear that changes over time are partly due to forgetting, but are by no means a simple function of forgetting, the general problem of decay is nevertheless little understood at present. A successful attack on understanding the determinants of persistence would seem to call for a closer integration between this kind of research on attitude change and research on the determinants of forgetting and retention originating in the experimental psychological laboratory (see, for example, Miller & Campbell, 1959), research on personality variables, and investigation of the effects of particular contents of persuasive communications.

Separating Critical Variables

Earlier we stressed the distinction between attention, comprehension, and acceptance. Variations in attention determine whether or not a communication reaches a person; variations in understanding and assimilating the information it contains determine whether it is potentially effective; when both attention and comprehension are held constant, its effectiveness will depend upon whether, for any number of other reasons, the recipient accepts it. The distinction is important because the variables which determine the effectiveness of a communication may affect these three stages of influence in varying ways and to different degrees; there are different implications for research depending on which of the processes one focuses on. In some investigations (such as the sleeper effect), separation of the effects due to learning from those due to acceptance are critical, and in other situations (for example fear-appeals), attention may increase while acceptance nevertheless decreases. The identification of these different factors as determinants of change is important, but it should be accompanied by an analysis of the psychological processes which underlie them and coordinated with the approaches which stress the notion of cognitive consistency (see Chs. 5 and 6). Beginnings in this direction are represented by the work of Brehm and Cohen (1962), Hovland and Rosenberg (1960), Katz (1960), and Kelman (1961).

Attitude and Behavior

Most of the investigators whose work we have examined make the broad psychological assumption that since attitudes are evaluative predispositions, they have consequences for the way people act toward others, for the programs they actually undertake, and for the manner in which they carry them out. Thus attitudes are always seen as precursors of behavior, as determinants of how a person will actually behave in his daily affairs. In spite of the wide acceptance of the assumption, however, very little work on attitude change has dealt explicitly with the behavior that may follow a change in attitude. Research workers have usually been content to demonstrate that there are factors which affect attitude change and that these factors are open to orderly exploration, without actually carrying through to the point where they examine the links between changed attitudes and changes in learning, performance, perception, and interaction. Until experimental research demonstrates that attitude change has consequences for subsequent behavior, we cannot be certain that our procedures for inducing change do anything more than cause cognitive realignments; perhaps we cannot even be certain that the concept of attitude has critical significance for psychology.

Conclusion

The problems needing investigation and the current efforts to explore them constitute a search for the processes mediating between the variables assumed to influence attitude change and the amount or kind of attitude change. The many psychological factors discussed in this book can be viewed as parts of the progressive specification of processes going on within the person between the time a persuasive stimulus enters his psychological field and the time his attitudes undergo a resultant change.

The next steps in the broad attack on attitude change require the integration of different assumed mediating processes into more inclusive systems which can explain with increasing accuracy larger and larger sets of phenomena. From such attempts at integration, new and more general insights will themselves stimulate new and interesting research. The task has only begun to be carried out in psychology as different theoretical and experimental traditions converge—for example, in the research programs which combine the Gestalt tradition of cognitive consistency with the behavioristic tradition of reinforcement of responses.

The degree to which new, more powerful theoretical formulations will be achieved is intimately connected with the design of the research used to test different combinations of theoretical assumptions. This chapter discussed earlier the differences between survey and experimental approaches, but here the question is the complexities of the controlled experimental design itself. Where research designs seek conclusions about a single variable without respect to other variables with which it might interact, the conclusions must be checked against a variety of experimental stimuli and under a variety of conditions before their generality can be assessed. Considering the complexity of the variables affecting attitude change, it is unlikely that there will be many generalizations that can be applied to all communication stimuli, to all recipients, and to all conditions under which the stimuli are presented. In the social world variables interact, and the effects of any one variable in producing attitude change may have to be specified differentially in terms of accompanying variables. Thus, if a conclusion about a single variable aims at generality, it is likely that it will have to dispense with the notion of a single principle in favor of a series of principles. These principles, however, may in turn all be related to one another by means of an over-all theoretical model.

Progress in research is guided by and benefits from being based on adequate theory. The development of a theoretical structure makes it increasingly likely that the experimenter can select beforehand the appropriate variables that affect the acceptance of a communication. It is easy to see why the old scientific adage "Any theory is better than none" continues to have currency among scientific investigators in spite of being a timeworn cliché. The advantage of a theory emphasizes again the desirability of integrating research on the effects of persuasive communications with basic research on the general psychological processes of motivation, perception, cognition, and learning. Even in the pursuit of practical knowledge, the decisions one can make on the basis of principles derived from a theoretical model are more effective, because they are more general and are not limited to instances of the phenomenon observed only at a given time. Another cliché is relevant here: "Good theory is most practical." In view of the fact that our ultimate objective in developing general principles is to increase our ability to understand concrete instances and to improve our capacity to make practical decisions, these old saws retain their vigor and significance for the psychologist.

Thus, the application of theory results in an enhanced understanding of what actually goes on in a real-life situation and has implications for practical action with regard to it. By working back and forth in this manner, we can illuminate many of the factors producing attitude change and at the same time emerge with new hypotheses and further directions for theoretical investigation. The increasingly more complicated spiral of theory, hypothesis, research, application, and new theory represents the best strategy for uncovering the psychological processes underlying attitude change and social influence.

REFERENCES

Adams, J. S. (1961). Reduction of cognitive dissonance by seeking consonant information. *Journal of Abnormal and Social Psychology*, 62, 74-78.

Adorno, T. W., Else Frenkel-Brunswik, D. J. Levinson, and R. N. Sanford (1950). *The Authoritarian Personality*. New York: Harper & Brothers.

Allyn, Jane, and Leon Festinger (1961). The effectiveness of unanticipated persuasive communications. *Journal of Abnormal and Social Psychology*, 62, 35-40.

Anderson, N. H., and A. A. Barrios (1961). Primacy effects in personality impression formation. *Journal of Abnormal and Social Psychology*, 63, 346-350.

Aronson, Elliot, and J. M. Carlsmith (1963). Effect of the severity of threat on the devaluation of forbidden behavior. *Journal of Abnormal and Social Psychology*, 66, 584-588.

Aronson, Elliot, and B. W. Golden (1962). The effect of relevant and irrelevant aspects of communicator credibility on opinion change. *Journal of Personality*, 30, 135-146.

Aronson, Elliot, and Judson Mills (1959). The effect of severity of initiation on liking for a group. *Journal of Abnormal and Social Psychology*, 59, 177-181.

Aronson, Elliot, Judith A. Turner, and J. M. Carlsmith (1963). Communicator credibility and communication discrepancy as determinants of opinion change. *Journal of Abnormal and Social Psychology*, 67, 31-36.

Asch, S. E. (1951). Effects of group pressure upon the modification and distortion of judgments. In Harold Guetzkow, ed., *Groups, Leadership and Men*. Pittsburgh: Carnegie Press. Pp. 177-190.

Baron, R. M. (1963). A cognitive model of attitude change. Unpublished doctoral dissertation, New York University.

Bennett, Edith B. (1955). Discussion, decision, commitment and consensus in "Group decision." *Human Relations*, 8, 251-273.

Berelson, B. R., P. F. Lazarsfeld, and W. N. McPhee (1954). *Voting: A Study of Opinion Formation in a Presidential Campaign*. Chicago: University of Chicago Press.

Berg, I. A., and B. M. Bass, eds. (1961). *Conformity and Deviation.* New York: Harper & Brothers.

Bergin, A. E. (1962). The effect of dissonant persuasive communications upon changes in a self-referring attitude. *Journal of Personality*, 30, 423-438.

Brehm, J. W. (1959). Increasing cognitive dissonance by a *fait accompli.* *Journal of Abnormal and Social Psychology*, 58, 379-382.

Brehm, J. W. (1960). Attitudinal consequences of commitment to unpleasant behavior. *Journal of Abnormal and Social Psychology*, 60, 379-383.

Brehm, J. W., and A. R. Cohen (1959). Choice and chance relative deprivation as determinants of cognitive dissonance. *Journal of Abnormal and Social Psychology*, 58, 383-387.

Brehm, J. W., and A. R. Cohen (1962). *Explorations in Cognitive Dissonance.* New York: John Wiley & Sons.

Brock, T. C. (1962). Cognitive restructuring and attitude change. *Journal of Abnormal and Social Psychology*, 64, 264-271.

Brock, T. C., and J. E. Blackwood (1962). Dissonance reduction, social comparison, and modification of others' opinions. *Journal of Abnormal and Social Psychology*, 65, 319-324.

Brock, T. C., and A. H. Buss (1962). Dissonance, aggression, and evaluation of pain. *Journal of Abnormal and Social Psychology*, 65, 197-202.

Brown, R. W. (1962). Models of attitude change. In R. W. Brown, Eugene Galanter, E. H. Hess, and George Mandler, *New Directions in Psychology.* New York: Holt, Rinehart and Winston. Pp. 3-85.

Carlson, E. R. (1956). Attitude change through modification of attitude structure. *Journal of Abnormal and Social Psychology*, 52, 256-261.

Cohen, A. R. (1957). Need for cognition and order of communication as determinants of opinion change. In C. I. Hovland, ed., *The Order of Presentation in Persuasion.* New Haven, Conn.: Yale University Press. Pp. 79-97.

Cohen, A. R. (1959a). Some implications of self-esteem for social influence. In C. I. Hovland and I. L. Janis, eds., *Personality and Persuasibility.* New Haven, Conn.: Yale University Press. Pp. 102-120.

Cohen, A. R. (1959b). Communication discrepancy and attitude change: a dissonance theory approach. *Journal of Personality*, 27, 386-396.

Cohen, A. R., J. W. Brehm, and W. H. Fleming (1958). Attitude change and justification for compliance. *Journal of Abnormal and Social Psychology*, 56, 276-278.

Cohen, A. R., H. I. Terry, and C. B. Jones (1959). Attitudinal effects of choice in exposure to counterpropaganda. *Journal of Abnormal and Social Psychology*, 58, 388-391.

Culbertson, Frances M. (1957). Modification of an emotionally held attitude through role-playing. *Journal of Abnormal and Social Psychology*, 54, 230-233.

Davis, K. E., and E. E. Jones (1960). Changes in interpersonal perception as a means of reducing cognitive dissonance. *Journal of Abnormal and Social Psychology*, 61, 402-410.

Deutsch, Morton, and Mary E. Collins (1951). *Interracial Housing: A Psychological Evaluation of a Social Experiment.* Minneapolis: University of Minnesota Press.

Deutsch, Morton, and H. B. Gerard (1955). A study of normative and informational social influences upon individual judgment. *Journal of Abnormal and Social Psychology*, 51, 629-636.

Ehrlich, Danuta, Isaiah Guttman, Peter Schönbach, and Judson Mills (1957). Postdecision exposure to relevant information. *Journal of Abnormal and Social Psychology*, 54, 98-102.

Emerson, R. M. (1954). Deviation and rejection: an experimental replication. *American Sociological Review*, 19, 688-692.

Festinger, Leon (1954). A theory of social comparison processes. *Human Relations*, 7, 117-140.

Festinger, Leon (1955). Social psychology and group processes. In C. P. Stone and Quinn McNemar, eds., *Annual Review of Psychology*, Vol. 6. Stanford, Calif.: Annual Reviews. Pp. 187-216.

Festinger, Leon (1957). *A Theory of Cognitive Dissonance.* Evanston, Ill.: Row, Peterson.

Festinger, Leon, and J. M. Carlsmith (1959). Cognitive consequences of forced compliance. *Journal of Abnormal and Social Psychology*, 58, 203-210.

Festinger, Leon, and Nathan Maccoby (1964). On resistance to persuasive communications. *Journal of Abnormal and Social Psychology*, 68, 359-366.

Fisher, Seymour, and Ardie Lubin (1958). Distance as a determinant of influence in a two-person serial interaction situation. *Journal of Abnormal and Social Psychology*, 56, 230-238.

Freedman, J. L. (1961). The effect of involvement on concept maintenance. Unpublished doctoral dissertation, Yale University.

Gardner, R. W., P. S. Holzman, G. S. Klein, Harriet Linton, and D. P. Spence (1959). Cognitive control: a study of individual consistencies in cognitive behavior. *Psychological Issues*, 1, No. 4.

Gerard, H. B. (1954). The anchorage of opinions in face-to-face groups. *Human Relations*, 7, 313-325.

Gerard, H. B. (1961a). Disagreement with others, their credibility, and experienced stress. *Journal of Abnormal and Social Psychology*, 62, 559-564.

Gerard, H. B. (1961b). Inconsistency of beliefs and their implications. Paper read at the Sixty-Ninth Annual Convention of the American Psychological Association, New York.

Goldberg, S. C. (1954). Three situational determinants of conformity to social norms. *Journal of Abnormal and Social Psychology*, 49, 325-329.

Goldstein, M. J. (1959). The relationship between coping and avoiding behavior and response to fear-arousing propaganda. *Journal of Abnormal and Social Psychology*, 58, 247-252.

Heider, Fritz (1958). *The Psychology of Interpersonal Relations*. New York: John Wiley & Sons.

Hildum, D. C., and R. W. Brown (1956). Verbal reinforcement and interviewer bias. *Journal of Abnormal and Social Psychology*, 53, 108-111.

Hochbaum, G. M. (1954). The relation between group members' self-confidence and their reactions to group pressures to uniformity. *American Sociological Review*, 6, 678-687.

Hovland, C. I., ed. (1957). *The Order of Presentation in Persuasion*. New Haven, Conn.: Yale University Press.

Hovland, C. I. (1959). Reconciling conflicting results derived from experimental and survey studies of attitude change. *American Psychologist*, 14, 8-17.

Hovland, C. I., O. J. Harvey, and Muzafer Sherif (1957). Assimilation and contrast effects in reactions to communication and attitude change. *Journal of Abnormal and Social Psychology*, 55, 244-252.

Hovland, C. I., and I. L. Janis, eds. (1959). *Personality and Persuasibility*. New Haven, Conn.: Yale University Press.

Hovland, C. I., I. L. Janis, and H. H. Kelley (1953). *Communication and Persuasion*. New Haven, Conn.: Yale University Press.

Hovland, C. I., A. A. Lumsdaine, and F. D. Sheffield (1949). *Experiments on Mass Communication*. Princeton, N.J.: Princeton University Press.

Hovland, C. I., and Wallace Mandell (1952). An experimental comparison of conclusion-drawing by the communicator and by the audience. *Journal of Abnormal and Social Psychology*, 47, 581-588.

Hovland, C. I., and H. A. Pritzker (1957). Extent of opinion change as a function of amount of change advocated. *Journal of Abnormal and Social Psychology*, 54, 257-261.

Hovland, C. I., and M. J. Rosenberg, eds. (1960). *Attitude Organization and Change*. New Haven, Conn.: Yale University Press.

Hovland, C. I., and Walter Weiss (1951). The influence of source credibility on communication effectiveness. *Public Opinion Quarterly*, 15, 635-650.

Hyman, H. H., and P. B. Sheatsley (1947). Some reasons why information campaigns fail. *Public Opinion Quarterly*, 11, 412-423.

Janis, I. L. (1957). Motivational effects of different sequential arrangements of conflicting arguments: a theoretical analysis. In C. I. Hovland, ed., *The Order of Presentation in Persuasion*. New Haven, Conn.: Yale University Press. Pp. 170-186.

Janis, I. L. (1958). *Psychological Stress*. New York: John Wiley & Sons.

Janis, I. L., and Seymour Feshbach (1953). Effects of fear-arousing communications. *Journal of Abnormal and Social Psychology*, 48, 78-92.

Janis, I. L., and B. T. King (1954). The influence of role-playing on opinion change. *Journal of Abnormal and Social Psychology*, 49, 211-218.

Janis, I. L., A. A. Lumsdaine, and A. I. Gladstone (1951). Effects of preparatory communications on reactions to a subsequent news event. *Public Opinion Quarterly*, 15, 487-518.

Janis, I. L., and H. C. Milholland, Jr. (1954). The influence of threat appeals on selective learning of the content of a persuasive communication. *Journal of Psychology*, 37, 75-80.

Janis, I. L., and R. F. Terwilliger (1962). An experimental study of psychological resistances to fear-arousing communications. *Journal of Abnormal and Social Psychology*, 65, 403-410.

Katz, Daniel, ed. (1960). Special issue on attitude change. *Public Opinion Quarterly*, 24, No. 2.

Katz, Daniel, Charles McClintock, and Irving Sarnoff (1957). The measurement of ego defense as related to attitude change. *Journal of Personality*, 25, 465-474.

Katz, Daniel, Irving Sarnoff, and Charles McClintock (1956). Ego-defense and attitude change. *Human Relations, 9*, 27-45.

Katz, Elihu (1957). The two-step flow of communication: an up-to-date report on an hypothesis. *Public Opinion Quarterly*, 21, 61-78.

Katz, Elihu, and P. F. Lazarsfeld (1955). *Personal Influence: The Part Played by People in the Flow of Mass Communications*. Glencoe, Ill.: Free Press.

Kelley, H. H., and T. W. Lamb (1957). Certainty of judgment and resistance to social influence. *Journal of Abnormal and Social Psychology*, 55, 137-139.

Kelley, H. H., and E. H. Volkhart (1952). The resistance to change of group-anchored attitudes. *American Sociological Review*, 17, 453-465.

Kelley, H. H., and Christine L. Woodruff (1956). Members' reactions to apparent group approval of a counternorm communication. *Journal of Abnormal and Social Psychology*, 52, 67-74.

Kelman, H. C. (1953). Attitude change as a function of response restriction. *Human Relations, 6*, 185-214.

Kelman, H. C. (1961). Processes of opinion change. *Public Opinion Quarterly*, 25, 57-78.

Kelman, H. C., and Jonas Cohler (1959). Reactions to persuasive communications as a function of cognitive needs and styles. Paper read at the Thirtieth Annual Meeting of the Eastern Psychological Association, Atlantic City, N.J.

Kelman, H. C., and C. I. Hovland (1953). "Reinstatement" of the communicator in delayed measurement of opinion change. *Journal of Abnormal and Social Psychology*, 48, 327-335.

King, B. T., and I. L. Janis (1956). Comparison of the effectiveness of improvised versus non-improvised role-playing in producing opinion changes. *Human Relations, 9,* 177-186.

Klapper, J. T. (1960). *The Effects of Mass Communication.* Glencoe, Ill.: Free Press.

Klein, G. S. (1958). Cognitive control and motivation. In Gardner Lindzey, ed., *Assessment of Human Motives.* New York: Rinehart and Company.

Krech, David, R. S. Crutchfield, and E. L. Ballachey (1962). *Individual in Society.* New York: McGraw-Hill Book Company.

Lana, R. E. (1961). Familiarity and the order of presentation of persuasive communications. *Journal of Abnormal and Social Psychology, 62,* 573-577.

Lazarsfeld, P. F., B. R. Berelson, and Hazel Gaudet (1948). *The People's Choice.* (2nd ed.) New York: Columbia University Press.

Leventhal, Howard, and S. I. Perloe (1962). A relationship between self-esteem and persuasibility. *Journal of Abnormal and Social Psychology, 64,* 385-388.

Lewan, P. C., and Ezra Stotland (1961). The effects of prior information on susceptibility to an emotional appeal. *Journal of Abnormal and Social Psychology, 62,* 450-453.

Lewin, Kurt (1943). Forces behind food habits and methods of change. *Bulletin of the National Research Council,* No. 108, 35-65.

Lipset, S. M., P. F. Lazarsfeld, A. H. Barton, and Juan Linz (1954). The psychology of voting: an analysis of political behavior. In Gardner Lindzey, ed., *Handbook of Social Psychology.* Reading, Mass.: Addison-Wesley Publishing Company. Pp. 1124-1175.

Lumsdaine, A. A., and I. L. Janis (1953). Resistance to "counter-propaganda" produced by one-sided and two-sided "propaganda" presentations. *Public Opinion Quarterly, 17,* 311-318.

Lund, F. H. (1925). The psychology of belief. IV. The law of primacy in persuasion. *Journal of Abnormal and Social Psychology, 20,* 183-191.

Manis, Melvin (1960). The interpretation of opinion statements as a function of recipient attitude. *Journal of Abnormal and Social Psychology, 60,* 340-344.

Manis, Melvin, and Joan B. Blake (1963). Interpretation of persuasive messages as a function of prior immunization. *Journal of Abnormal and Social Psychology, 66,* 225-230.

McGuire, W. J. (1961a). Resistance to persuasion conferred by active and passive prior refutation of the same and alternative counter-arguments. *Journal of Abnormal and Social Psychology, 63,* 326-332.

McGuire, W. J. (1961b). The effectiveness of supportive and refutational defenses in immunizing and restoring beliefs against persuasion. *Sociometry, 24,* 184-197.

McGuire, W. J. (1962). Persistence of the resistance to persuasion induced by various types of prior belief defenses. *Journal of Abnormal and Social Psychology*, 64, 241-248.

McGuire, W. J., and Demetrios Papageorgis (1961). The relative efficacy of various types of prior belief-defense in producing immunity against persuasion. *Journal of Abnormal and Social Psychology*, 62, 327-337.

McGuire, W. J., and Demetrios Papageorgis (1962). Effectiveness of forewarning in developing resistance to persuasion. *Public Opinion Quarterly*, 26, 24-34.

Menzel, Herbert, and Elihu Katz (1955). Social relations and innovation in the medical profession: the epidemiology of a new drug. *Public Opinion Quarterly*, 19, 337-352.

Miller, N. E. (1944). Experimental studies of conflict. In J. McV. Hunt, ed., *Personality and the Behavior Disorders*. New York: The Ronald Press. Pp. 431-465.

Miller, N. E. (1959). Liberalization of basic S-R concepts: extension to conflict behavior, motivation and social learning. In Sigmund Koch, ed., *Psychology: A Study of a Science*, Vol. 2. New York: McGraw-Hill Book Company. Pp. 196-292.

Miller, Norman, and D. T. Campbell (1959). Recency and primacy in persuasion as a function of the timing of speeches and measurements. *Journal of Abnormal and Social Psychology*, 59, 1-9.

Mills, Judson, Elliot Aronson, and Hal Robinson (1959). Selectivity in exposure to information. *Journal of Abnormal and Social Psychology*, 59, 250-253.

Mitnick, L. L., and Elliott McGinnies (1958). Influencing ethnocentrism in small discussion groups through a film communication. *Journal of Abnormal and Social Psychology*, 56, 82-90.

Osgood, C. E. (1960). Cognitive dynamics in the conduct of human affairs. *Public Opinion Quarterly*, 24, 341-365.

Papageorgis, Demetrios, and W. J. McGuire (1961). The generality of immunity to persuasion produced by pre-exposure to weakened counterarguments. *Journal of Abnormal and Social Psychology*, 62, 475-481.

Pennington, D. F., Jr., François Haravey, and B. M. Bass (1958). Some effects of decision and discussion on coalescence, change, and effectiveness. *Journal of Applied Psychology*, 42, 404-408.

Rabbie, J. M., J. W. Brehm, and A. R. Cohen (1959). Verbalization and reactions to cognitive dissonance. *Journal of Personality*, 27, 407-417.

Rhine, R. J. (1958). A concept formation approach to attitude acquisition. *Psychological Review*, 65, 362-370.

Rosen, Sidney (1961). Postdecision affinity for incompatible information. *Journal of Abnormal and Social Psychology*, 63, 188-190.

Rosenberg, M. J. (1956). Cognitive structure and attitudinal affect. *Journal of Abnormal and Social Psychology*, 53, 367-372.

Rosenberg, M. J. (1960). Cognitive reorganization in response to the hypnotic reversal of attitudinal affect. *Journal of Personality,* 28, 39-63.

Rosenberg, M. J., and R. P. Abelson (1960). An analysis of cognitive balancing. In C. I. Hovland and M. J. Rosenberg, eds., *Attitude Organization and Change.* New Haven, Conn.: Yale University Press. Pp. 112-163.

Sarnoff, Irving (1960a). Reaction formation and cynicism. *Journal of Personality,* 28, 129-143.

Sarnoff, Irving (1960b). Psychoanalytic theory and social attitudes. *Public Opinion Quarterly,* 24, 251-279.

Sarnoff, Irving, and S. M. Corwin (1959). Castration anxiety and the fear of death. *Journal of Personality,* 27, 374-385.

Sarnoff, Irving, and Daniel Katz (1954). The motivational bases of attitude change. *Journal of Abnormal and Social Psychology,* 49, 115-124.

Schachter, Stanley (1951). Deviation, rejection, and communication. *Journal of Abnormal and Social Psychology,* 46, 190-207.

Scott, W. A. (1956). The avoidance of threatening material in imaginative behavior. *Journal of Abnormal and Social Psychology,* 52, 338-346.

Scott, W. A. (1957). Attitude change through reward of verbal behavior. *Journal of Abnormal and Social Psychology,* 55, 72-75.

Scott, W. A. (1959a). Cognitive consistency, response reinforcement, and attitude change. *Sociometry,* 22, 219-229.

Scott, W. A. (1959b). Attitude change by response reinforcement: replication and extension. *Sociometry,* 22, 328-335.

Sherif, Muzafer (1935). A study of some social factors in perception. *Archives of Psychology,* 27, No. 187.

Sherif, Muzafer, and C. I. Hovland (1961). *Social Judgment.* New Haven, Conn.: Yale University Press.

Singer, R. D. (1961). Verbal conditioning and generalization of prodemocratic responses. *Journal of Abnormal and Social Psychology,* 63, 43-46.

Smith, E. E. (1961). The power of dissonance techniques to change attitudes. *Public Opinion Quarterly,* 25, 626-639.

Steiner, I. D. (1962). Receptivity to supportive versus nonsupportive communications. *Journal of Abnormal and Social Psychology,* 65, 266-267.

Tannenbaum, P. H. (1953). Attitudes toward source and concept as factors in attitude change through communications. Unpublished doctoral dissertation, University of Illinois.

Thistlethwaite, D. L., Henry de Haan, and Joseph Kamenetsky (1955). The effects of "directive" and "nondirective" communication procedures on attitudes. *Journal of Abnormal and Social Psychology,* 51, 107-113.

Thistlethwaite, D. L., and Joseph Kamenetsky (1955). Attitude change through refutation and elaboration of audience counterarguments. *Journal of Abnormal and Social Psychology*, 51, 3-12.

Upshaw, H. S. (1962). Own attitude as an anchor in equal-appearing intervals. *Journal of Abnormal and Social Psychology*, 64, 85-96.

Walker, E. L., and R. W. Heyns (1962). *An Anatomy for Conformity*. Englewood Cliffs, N.J.: Prentice-Hall.

Walster, Elaine, and Leon Festinger (1962). The effectiveness of "overheard" persuasive communications. *Journal of Abnormal and Social Psychology*, 65, 395-402.

Weiss, Walter (1953). A "sleeper" effect in opinion change. *Journal of Abnormal and Social Psychology*, 48, 173-180.

Weiss, Walter (1957). Opinion congruence with a negative source on one issue as a factor influencing agreement on another issue. *Journal of Abnormal and Social Psychology*, 54, 180-186.

Weiss, Walter (1961). The effects of a communication on attitude change and scale judgments. *Journal of Abnormal and Social Psychology*, 62, 133-140.

Weiss, Walter, and B. J. Fine (1955). Opinion change as a function of some intrapersonal attributes of the communicatees. *Journal of Abnormal and Social Psychology*, 51, 246-253.

Weiss, Walter, and B. J. Fine (1956). The effect of induced aggressiveness on opinion change. *Journal of Abnormal and Social Psychology*, 52, 109-114.

Weiss, Walter, and Bernhardt Lieberman (1959). The effects of "emotional" language on the induction and change of opinions. *Journal of Social Psychology*, 50, 129-141.

Wilner, D. M., Rosabelle P. Walkley, and S. W. Cook (1955). *Human Relations in Interracial Housing: A Study of the Contact Hypothesis*. Minneapolis: University of Minnesota Press.

Zimbardo, P. G. (1960). Involvement and communication discrepancy as determinants of opinion conformity. *Journal of Abnormal and Social Psychology*, 60, 86-94.

Zimbardo, P. G. (1963). Role playing: improvisation or dissonance? Unpublished paper, New York University.

INDEX